W9-ABZ-248

# The Non-- Designer's Type Book

## Second Edition

# The Non-Designer's Type Book

## Second Edition

Insights and techniques
for creating professional-level type

*Robin Williams*

Peachpit Press
Berkeley • California

**The Non-Designer's Type Book, second edition**
Robin Williams

Copyright © 2006 by Robin Williams
Cover illustration and cover design: John Tollett
Interior design and production: Robin Williams
Update assistance: Barbara Sikora
Editing: Nancy Davis

Peachpit Press
1249 Eighth Street
Berkeley, California 94710
800.283.9444
510.524.2178 phone
510.524.2221 fax

Find us on the web at www.peachpit.com
To report errors, please send a note to errata@peachpit.com

Peachpit Press is a division of Pearson Education
The appendix article "Listen to Your Eyes" was printed in
*Layers, The How-To Magazine for Everything Adobe,* July/
August 2005. Reprinted with permission.

The chapter "Telltale Signs of Desktop Publishing" was
originally printed in slightly altered form in *Adobe Magazine,*
July/August 1995 under the title "Thirteen Telltale Signs."
©1995 Adobe Systems, Inc., all rights reserved.

**ISBN 0-321-30336-9**
10 9 8 7 6 5 4 3 2 1
Printed and bound in the United States of America

To Allan Haley
with grateful appreciation
for inspiring, educating,
and befriending me.

I advise the layperson
to spread India ink
on an uncarved board,
lay paper on top of it,
and print it.
He will get a black print,
but the result is not
the blackness of ink,
it is the blackness of prints.

Now the object
is to give this print
greater life and greater power
by carving its surface.
Whatever I carve
I compare with an uncarved print
and ask myself,
"Which has more beauty,
more strength,
more depth,
more magnitude,
more movement,
more tranquility?"

If there is anything here
that is inferior to an uncarved block,
then I have not created my print,
I have lost to the block.

Shiko Munakata

# Contents

## Typographic Choices

## Glossary of Type Terms

## Other Info

The trumpet don't make the music
and the computer don't make the type.
You can put a cat in the oven
but that don't make it a biscuit.

# Introduction

With the advent of computers on the desktop in the late twentieth century, type and typography reached new heights of popularity. With this increased awareness has come increased sophistication and the need for the average person to understand how to create beautiful, professional typography that emphasizes the message, typography that is pleasing to the reader, and that invites readers in and keeps them there.

If you have read and followed the guidelines in *The Mac is not a typewriter* or *The PC is not a typewriter,* you are already creating type on a more professional level than you were before. Most of the techniques in this book can only be accomplished in a page layout application such as Adobe InDesign, Adobe PageMaker, or QuarkXPress. This book takes you several steps beyond those basic guidelines that you might have used in a word processor, into more subtle details that make the difference between good and sophisticated. You already recognize the difference—I'm sure you can glance at the two samples on the following page and instantly give an opinion as to which one is of higher quality. But can you name exactly what is creating that difference? Some differences are easily identified, others are more subtle. All are important.

If you're creating web pages, you'll find that many of the most important typographic techniques cannot be accomplished in the plain text on a web page. Type on the web will grow more sophisticated in the future, but for now many of the special techniques can only be applied to web pages as graphic pieces of type; that is, you create the headlines or fancy type in a graphics application, then put that graphic onto the web page. When you make that graphic text, you should of course apply every professional technique available.

Some of the guidelines in this book are too time-consuming for many everyday jobs, and I don't want you to think that unless you follow every suggestion here, your type will be inferior. But a key to creating great type is knowing what the options are in the first place. Once you know them, you can make choices as to when it might be appropriate to forgo some of the finer features.

So spend a couple of moments with the next few pages, make yourself conscious of the details, and see how many differences you can name before you look at the list. Then onward through the rest of the book, gleefully!

. . . . . . . . . . . . . . . . . . . . . . . . . . . . . . . . . . . . . . . . . . . .

# Training your eye

Glance quickly at the two quotations set below, and be conscious of your instant reaction as to which one has a more sophisticated appearance. Then look more closely at the one on the left, and see how many details you can pinpoint that contribute to its unprofessional appearance. Then look carefully at the quotation on the right, and see how many differences you can spot. Each of those differences helps to create the cleaner and more sophisticated appeal of the second quotation setting.

"HUMAN SOCIETY, the world, man in his entirety is in the alphabet. The alphabet is a source...first comes the house of man and its construction, then the human body, its build and deformities; then justice, music, the church; war, harvest, geometry; the mountain, nomadic life and secluded life, astronomy, toil and rest; the horse and the snake; the hammer and the urn which--turned over and struck--makes a bell; trees, rivers, roads; and finally destiny and God.

That is what the alphabet signifies."

--*Victor Hugo*, 1802-1885

"HUMAN SOCIETY, the world, man in his entirety is in the alphabet. The alphabet is a source . . . first comes the house of man and its construction, then the human body, its build and deformities; then justice, music, the church; war, harvest, geometry; the mountain, nomadic life and secluded life, astronomy, toil and rest; the horse and the snake; the hammer and the urn which—turned over and struck—makes a bell; trees, rivers, roads; and finally destiny and God.

"That is what the alphabet signifies."

~*Victor Hugo*, 1802–1885

. . . . . . . . . . . . . . . . . . . . . . . . . . . . . . . . . . . . . . . . . . . . . . . . . . . .

| Wrong | Better |
|---|---|
| The 12-point type is large and clunky. | The 10-point type is easier to read because you can see entire phrases, plus it has a more sophisticated look. (p. 193) |
| The line length is too short to justify the size of the text, creating uneven word spacing and too many hyphenated words. | Setting the type flush left instead of justified ensures that there is even spacing between the words. (pp. 38, 123) |
| The quote marks are ditto marks, not true quotation marks. And the first "quote" mark makes the text appear to indent in the first line. | The quotation marks are true quote marks, and the first one is hung into the margin, eliminating the appearance of an indent. (pp. 53, 57) |
| The computer ellipsis (…) is too tight. | The ellipsis is set with thin spaces and periods for more elegant spacing. (pp.66–67) |
| Double-hyphens are used instead of em dashes. | Em dashes are used instead of double hyphens. (p. 68) |
| The paragraph space is created by hitting two Returns, making much too much space between paragraphs. | The space between paragraphs is only half a line space, maintaining a closer connection between paragraphs. (p. 118) |
| There are two-letter hyphenations. And the last paragraph has the worst sort of widow (a hyphenated last word). | Hyphenations have been eliminated. (p. 148) |
| There is a hyphen between the dates instead of an en dash. | Oldstyle figures are used for the dates, separated by an en dash. The baseline shift of the en dash was adjusted. (p. 72) |
| The small caps are computer generated, creating a discrepancy between the stroke weights of the small caps and those of the other letters and the capital. | The small caps in the first line are true-drawn. (p. 91) |
| The byline (Victor Hugo) is italic, so the comma after his name should also be italic, not roman. (p. 67)<br><br>*Technically, the phrase does not need quotation marks around it, but I wanted to display them. When more than one paragraph is quoted, the proper convention is to place quotation marks at the **beginning** of each paragraph, but only at the **end** of the **last** paragraph.* | In the byline, an ornament has been used instead of a dash. (pp. 163–164)<br><br>Swash characters were used for the first letters of Victor Hugo's name. These are not only a subtle visual pleasure, but also prevent the italic V from bumping into the dot on the lowercase i. (p. 151–154)<br><br>Auto pair kerning has been used. Manual kerning has been used, where necessary. (pp. 107–111) Where appropriate, ligatures have been used. (pp. 95–96) |

BOLDNESS HAS GENIUS,
POWER,
AND MAGIC IN IT.

Goethe

# Review

This book is meant to follow *The Mac is not a typewriter* or *The PC is not a typewriter*. Rather than repeat everything I wrote in those first books, I must assume you have read it and are following those basic typographic principles. But just in case you think you're ready for this book without having read the other, I am including here a brief review. If you answer no (**N**) to any of these points, please take a few moments to read *The Mac/PC is not a typewriter*.

**Y N**    I type *one* space after periods, commas, colons, semicolons, exclamation points, question marks, parentheses, and any other punctuation.

**Y N**    I *always* use true quotation marks ("”), *never* dumb ol' ditto marks (" ").

**Y N**    I *always* use true apostrophes (' not '), and I *always* put them in the right places.

**Y N**    I know the differences between hyphens, en dashes, and em dashes; when to use each; and how to type them.

**Y N**    I know how to use Special Characters on my Macintosh or the Character Map on my PC to access special characters such as ©, ™, ¢, ®, £, or €.

**Y N**    I know how to place accent marks over the appropriate letters, as in résumé.

**Y N**    I know to *never* underline text.

**Y N**    I *rarely* use all caps, and when I do it is certainly not under the mistaken assumption that all caps are easier to read.

**Y N**    I *always* avoid leaving widows and orphans on the page.

In this book I elaborate on some of the information that's presented in *The Mac/PC is not a typewriter*, but the material in this volume is very different from that in the previous books. If necessary, run down to your library, find *The Mac/PC is not a typewriter*, and take twenty minutes to get the gist of it. Especially if you're still typing two spaces after periods.

*Robin*

# Anatomy of type

Before we begin, let's look at a few characters up close so when you read specific typographic terms throughout the rest of the book, you'll know what I'm talking about.

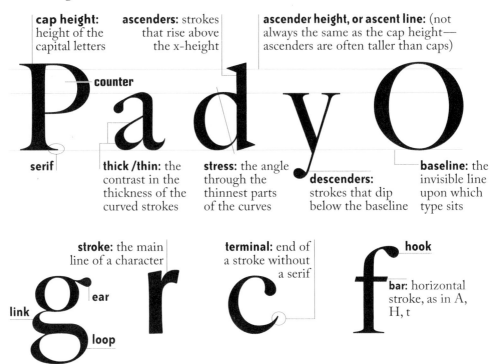

**cap height:** height of the capital letters

**ascenders:** strokes that rise above the x-height

**ascender height, or ascent line:** (not always the same as the cap height— ascenders are often taller than caps)

counter

serif

**thick /thin:** the contrast in the thickness of the curved strokes

**stress:** the angle through the thinnest parts of the curves

**descenders:** strokes that dip below the baseline

**baseline:** the invisible line upon which type sits

**stroke:** the main line of a character

**terminal:** end of a stroke without a serif

hook

link

ear

loop

**bar:** horizontal stroke, as in A, H, t

SERIF
**SANS**

*Serif type has "serifs," as circled above. "Sans" is French for "without," so "sans serif" type has no serifs.*

a*a*   *ff*   *gg*   h*h*
aa   ff   gg   hh

Notice how the serif letter **a** changes from a "two-story" **a** into a "one-story" *a* when it is italic, but the sans serif does not. That is typical of how the design of most serifs and sans serifs change when italic (but not all).

**body copy:** Text in sizes from about 8- to 12-point, set in paragraphs, as shown here (this is 10-point type).

**display type:** Text in sizes above 14 point, as in headlines or advertising titles. Shown above is 90-point display type.

**roman:** Type that does not slant. This type you're reading is roman.

**italic:** A style of type where the letters slant to the right. Most serif faces have true italic versions—the letters have been redesigned. See the comparisons (to the left) of the roman and italic versions of the same typeface.

**oblique:** The type is just slanted. This is typical of most sans serif "italic" faces (but not all).

## The x-height

The x-height of a typeface is the size of the body of the characters as epitomized by the letter x, since x is the only letter that reaches out to all four corners of the space.

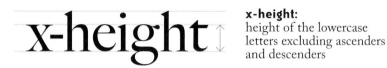

**x-height:**
height of the lowercase
letters excluding ascenders
and descenders

It is the x-height that creates the impression of the font's size. You see, the point size of the type as you know it, let's say 24 point, originally referred to the size of the little piece of metal on which the letter was created. Within that 24-point space, the designer could do anything he wanted—he could make tall ascenders, a large x-height, a small x-height, short descenders. He didn't even have to take up the whole 24-point space. So when we say a typeface is a certain point size, we are really only getting an approximation of the actual number of points from the top of the character's ascenders to the bottom of its descenders. And even if the actual measurement from top to bottom is the same in several typefaces, the x-height varies widely. Since most of what you see of a typeface is the x-height, it is that which gives a face its visual impact.

Every one of the fonts shown below is set in 24-point type. You can see how radically the x-height changes the impression, even though most of the capital letters are relatively the same size. Be conscious of the x-height in the fonts you use—you will make some typographic decisions, such as linespacing, point size for body copy, and readability enhancement based on the x-height of the typeface.

Typed  Typed  Typed  **Typed**

Typed  *Typed*  Typed  Typed

*These are all 24-point type.*

. . . . . . . . . . . . . . . . . . . . . . . . . . . . . . . . . . . . . . . . . . . . . . . . . . . . . . . . . . . . .

# Points and picas

When you're working with type, you need to work in points and picas. It's just like using inches and feet, but the sizes are smaller—there are 12 inches in a foot; there are 12 points in a pica. But like I said, points and picas are much smaller—6 picas in 1 inch (which makes 72 points, then, in one inch).

Even if you've never formally worked with points before, you have a pretty good idea about how big 10-point type is as opposed to 24-point type because you choose and use point sizes of type on your computer all the time. So don't get nervous, just be conscious about those tiny sizes and try to use them more often. When your software, for instance, gives you a choice of using points or inches or lines, try using points. Once you start doing it, you'll probably find that it is actually easier to use points. I have a much clearer idea of how much space will be between the paragraphs if I ask for 6 points than if I ask for .083 inches. And I get confused about whether .083 inches is more or less than .072 inches, but I know darn well that 10 points is more than 8 points. Try dividing an 11-inch page into thirds. Ha! But change the measurement to picas, and the page is 66 picas, which is much easier to divide into thirds.

In general, we measure type sizes in points, and the space between lines or paragraphs in points. When measuring distances, such as the length of a line or the depth of a block of text, we use picas. Combining the two measurements is just like combining feet and inches: just as we write 6′2″ (6 feet, 2 inches), we write 3p4 (3 picas, 4 points).

Just so you know, traditionally (before desktop publishing) 72 points did not equal *exactly* 1 inch (it was a tiny smidgeon off). But when the Macintosh was originally created with a screen resolution of exactly 72 pixels per inch, our measurements for points became, on the Mac and then later on the PC, exactly 72 points per inch. Some software will let you override this standard, computerized amount and change it back to the traditional amount, but it's just about never necessary to do that.

# A Brief History of Type

In which we briefly explore
the history of the world and
how it affects typography,
and how this in turn affects
your typographic choices.
Don't skip this chapter—
many references will be made
to the categories of type
as described herein.

Type is one of the most
eloquent means of expression
in every epoch of style.
Next to architecture,
it gives the most characteristic portrait
of a period and the most severe testimony
of a nation's intellectual status.

❧ Peter Behrens

# Centuries of Type

The number of digitized typefaces is astounding, numbering well past 100,000 at the moment. It can be an overwhelming experience to decide which ones to buy, or even which ones to use.

However, if you group typefaces that have similar characteristics into a small number of categories, it makes the selection process much more manageable— it's easier to choose the typefaces you need to buy for your library by choosing a few from each category, and it's easier to decide which combination of faces to use on the page by making sure you grab no more than one from each category. And the process of grouping fonts makes you notice their more subtle features, makes you become more intimately involved.

It makes about as much sense to group several thousand faces into seven categories as it does to group human personalities into several character "types." There are always typefaces (or humans) with little quirks that prevent them from being conveniently pigeonholed, but there are generally enough shared characteristics in type to make it worth the effort.

I'm going to talk about seven different categories: oldstyle, modern, slab serif, sans serif, fringe/distressed, script, and decorative. The first five groups follow a historical perspective—there are interesting parallels between type development and developments in other areas of civilization such as architecture, arche-ology, philosophy, even economics. This doesn't mean that every typeface in a category was developed at that point in history. Goudy Oldstyle, designed by Frederic Goudy in 1915, is a classic example of the oldstyle category which began developing around 1500. The printer Aldus Manutius is credited with cutting the first oldstyle type in 1495; in fact, Aldus was such an important character that I have reprinted a story about him at the end of this chapter.

. . . . . . . . . . . . . . . . . . . . . . . . . . . . . . . . . . . . . . . . . . . . . . . . . .

# Oldstyle

The characteristics of the oldstyle typefaces originally developed out of the traditional handlettering form, following the way the scribes held the pens and drew letters. When moveable type was developed in the mid 1400s, the letterforms that were carved out of metal resembled what everyone was familiar with—letters formed with a broad-tipped pen held at an angle. At that point in history, the only printed material was books. Big books. Books that sat on lecterns and were read aloud from. Since the only project for a printing press was to create books (there were no business cards or bread wrappers yet), the first typefaces were eminently *readable* because that was their only job.

Oldstyle typefaces tend to have a warm, graceful appearance and are the best choice for setting readable, lengthy bodies of text. Classic oldstyles are among the most "invisible," meaning that the character forms don't interrupt the communication; usually there are no design characteristics that trip your eye. The main body text you're reading right now is set in a classic oldstyle called Caslon (Adobe Caslon Pro).

Oldstyle typefaces always have serifs. The serifs on the lowercase letters slant and are "bracketed," meaning the serifs connect to the main strokes with a curve. The strokes make a gentle transition from thick to thin, as the broad pen made naturally. And if you draw a line through the thinnest parts of the rounded forms of a letter, the line is diagonal—this is called the "stress"; oldstyle faces have a diagonal stress.

# Caslon   Minion   *Oldstyle typefaces*
# Bembo   Times   *Note the diagonal stress*
# Palatino Garamond

· · · · · · · · · · · · · · · · · · · · · · · · · · · · · · · · · · · · · · · · · · · · · · · · · ·

# Modern

Times changed. The world changed. Type changed. Typefaces in the modern style were developed at a time when people were beginning to view the world differently. America ushered in democracy, France ushered out monarchy, the Industrial Revolution was underway, and political and social theorists were establishing a more rational, mechanical view of the universe and its inhabitants. Baroque, rococo, and oldstyle faces were rendered obsolete. Modern type reflected strict emphasis on structure and form, and the last vestige of type's handwritten origins disappeared.

Modern typefaces have a sparkle and an elegance, but they also tend to have a severe and cold appearance. They are not very *readable;* that is, they are not often the best choice for *lengthy* or small text, as the strong thick/thin contrast creates an effect called "dazzling" that is hard on the eyes.

Modern faces have serifs, but the serifs on all characters are horizontal and very thin, with little or no bracketing (there is no curve where the serif meets the stroke). The strokes that create the letterforms change radically from thick to thin. The stress is now absolutely vertical.

# Onyx  Didot          *Modern typefaces*

# Bodoni  *Note the vertical stress*

# Bodoni Poster

· · · · · · · · · · · · · · · · · · · · · · · · · · · · · · · · · · · · · · · · · · · · · · · · · · ·

# Slab serif

Well, the Industrial Revolution really got going, and one of the results was a new field of business: advertising. Until then, of course, there were very few products to advertise. At first type designers tried to fatten up the thick strokes of the moderns, but the excessively strong combination of very fat strokes with very thin strokes made the text almost impossible to read. So they fattened up the entire letterform.

Slab serif typefaces also have serifs, and the serifs are horizontal, but they're thick. Fat. Slabs. The strokes that create the letterforms may make a very slight transition from thick to thin, or there may be no transition at all in some faces. The stress, when there is any, is vertical. Slab serif typefaces have a more regimented and strong appearance than do oldstyles.

I'll bet you were wondering why so many slab serif fonts are not named after their designers. Many of the *oldstyle* faces are named for their designers, such as Goudy and Baskerville and Garamond, but many *slab serifs* are named with Egyptian references such as Scarab, Memphis, Nile, and Glypha. It's indirectly because of Napoleon. One of his engineers found the Rosetta Stone, which turned out to be the key that unlocked the ancient hieroglyphics. This created a worldwide interest in Egyptian archeology and a mania for anything Egyptian. Type foundries noticed that if they named their typeface with an Egyptian reference, it sold better. To this day this category of type is sometimes called "Egyptian," even though there is no correlation between the style and the country except a fad. Slab serifs are also called "Clarendons" because the Clarendon typeface is the quintessential example of this category, as shown below.

**Clarendon**     *Slab serif typefaces*

Memphis

New Century Schoolbook

Candida, **Candida Bold**

· · · · · · · · · · · · · · · · · · · · · · · · · · · · · · · · · · · · · · · · · · · · · · · · ·

## Sans serif

In 1816 William Caslon IV created a "two-line Egyptian" typeface in which he took off all the serifs because he hated slab serifs. This face was not a big hit. It wasn't until the Bauhaus school of design was formed in 1919 that sans serifs (typefaces without serifs; "sans" is French for "without") began to be popular. Under the Bauhaus motto of "form follows function," typefaces were stripped down to their bare essentials, to their simplest, most functional forms, epitomized in the font Futura. This new school of design influenced the world.

Sans serifs, of course, have no serifs at all. Also, the strokes that create the letterforms have almost no visible transition from thick to thin (there are a very few exceptions, such as the typeface Optima). Sans serifs tend to have very large x-heights and so present quite a presence on the page.

# Futura: form follows function

## Today Sans

*Sans serif typefaces*

## Formata  Trade Gothic

# Grunge or distressed type

With the advent of the Macintosh computers and desktop publishing, type design—for the first time on earth—was put into the hands of the masses. Even more important, I believe, is that a mass *interest* in type was sparked— many people who never noticed typefaces before were suddenly wondering about the fonts on billboards and bread wrappers. With the power to create personal typefaces and to manipulate their layout on the screen, all the rules of traditional design and typography can be demolished. Who knows where this typographic anarchy will lead, but it is certainly fun and exciting to watch (and to use!).

Fringe typefaces (also variously called distressed, grunge, garage, deconstructive, edge, lawless, or just plain ugly) are typically distorted, schizophrenic, deliberately trashed, often difficult to read. But they are certainly identifiable and different from any other typefaces in history, and many are exquisitely beautiful in their ugliness. And they are incredibly fun to use. You might want to check out an old book of mine called *A Blip in the continuum,* illustrated by John Tollett, that is simply a celebration of ugly type.

*Fringe typefaces—aren't they amazing? I love them.*

· · · · · · · · · · · · · · · · · · · · · · · · · · · · · · · · · · · · · · · · ·

## Scripts

Script and decorative typefaces have popped up in just about every period of typographic history. Script faces, of course, emulate handlettering in many varieties—blackletter (as in many of the Bibles handlettered by scribes), calligraphic (as in wedding invitations), drafting (as in architects' drawings), cartoon, and so on. No one has trouble identifying typefaces in this category.

*Lamar Pen*  *Script typefaces*

*Dorchester Script*  *Dear Sarah*

**Cocktail Shaker**  *Nuptial*

*Emmascript*  *Scriptorama*

## Decorative

Decoratives are quite noticeable as well—the fonts made of ballet shoes or rope or Japanese pagodas or eraser dust. Decorative faces are not meant for anything else except to be decorative, which is far from an idle occupation. They can add punch to a publication, create a definite "look," or emphasize the content. If overused, they can destroy a design.

**Baileywick**  *Decorative typefaces*

Planet Serif  **Childa Dos**

**BILL'S FAT FREDDY**

Blue Island  Mister Frisky

# Aldus Manutius

AL   DVS

Have you ever wondered why roman type is called roman and italic type is called italic? Well, you can stop losing sleep over it.

Strange as it seems, in fifteenth-century Italy, land of the Romans, very few publications were printed with Roman letters—almost all scholarly or religious works were set in Greek. There weren't many other sorts of books anyway, except scholarly or religious works. Not many romance novels or horror stories.

When the man Aldus Manutius entered the publishing business with his company called the Dolphin Press, the printing industry was less than fifty years old. But there were already more than a thousand presses operating across Europe, and literally millions of books had been printed. Aldus was proud and protective of his Greek fonts, but a bit sloppy and diffident about his Roman fonts. In fact, most of them were not very well designed, and he used them only for jobs sponsored by wealthy clients or academic friends. In 1496, though, Aldus published an essay for Pietro Bembo, an Italian scholar and friend. The Bembo typeface, with its lighter weight, more pronounced weight stress, and more delicate serifs, was an instant success. Claude Garamond picked it up in France and spread its influence throughout the rest of Europe. This "Aldine roman" typeface, Bembo, affected type design for hundreds of years. (The body copy you are reading right now is set in Bembo.)

Aldus himself produced well over 1,200 different book titles in his 25 years as a publisher. Over 90 percent of the books he produced were Greek classics. Aldus was a well-patronized scholar before he entered the printing and publishing trade, so the classics were close to his heart. The market for his books was made up of the educated, the worldly, and the wealthy. Aldus created small books, or octavos, intended for busy people, for nobility traveling across Europe on errands of state, and for members of the "educational revolution" who were studying in the growing number of universities. Thus Aldus was the first creator of small, portable, "paperback" books.

The official writing style of the learned and professional scribes of southern Italy in the late 1400s was a relaxed, oblique, and flourishy script called *cancellaresca*. To make his books more appealing to the higher-class market, Aldus took this exclusive writing style and developed a typeface out of it. It was a hit. What a marketeer.

Aldus had his new type style copyrighted. He was trying to protect not just the one font—he wanted a monopoly on the cursive sort of style. He got it; he even got a papal decree to protect his rights. But as we all know, that doesn't mean no one will steal it. People did. At least the other Italians called the style "Aldino"; the rest of Europe called it "italic," since it came from Italy. The first italic Aldus ever cut (well, actually Francesco Griffo cut it) was produced in 1501 in Venice.

These innovations of Aldus Manutius place him in history as perhaps the most important printer of the Renaissance, next to Gutenberg himself. Popularizing the italic typeface, albeit inadvertently, had a profound influence on typeface development for generations. Prior to Aldus's beautiful octavos, the only small, portable books were prayer books; all other works were massive volumes that sat on lecterns for reading out loud. With the development of his italic type, more text could be set on a page, thus saving paper and space and making books more affordable. Education became more accessible, and the world changed. Again.

The function of reada-
bility
is often taken too liter-
ally
and over-emphasized
at the
cost of individuality.

Paul Rand

# Readability and Legibility

In which we come to
understand what makes
type readable or legible,
and how to improve the
readability or legibility
of typefaces in various
situations.

THERE ARE THOSE WHO CONTEND that culture alone dictates our reading preferences, and that readability is based not upon the intrinsic forms of the characters, but upon what we are *accustomed* to reading. Often cited as "proof" of this is the German preference for blackletter that continued centuries after the rest of the world had moved on to more sensible typefaces. Without proposing any scientific studies, I venture to suggest that just because someone *prefers* a particular typeface does not mean it is more *readable.* Your grandmother, I am sure, preferred that you send her a handwritten letter; in fact, she was probably offended if you wrote her a letter on a typewriter. Even though your typewritten letter would have been easier to read than your handwriting, Grandma was not basing her preference upon readability, but upon other, more emotional responses. And I would propose that the German preference for blackletter was not because the letterforms were easier for them to read than what the rest of the world was reading, but that they had some other bonding with the blackletter forms.

*Robin*

Dear Grandma,
I wish you would let me use my computer to write to you. These darn letters take me two weeks to prepare. C'mon, this blackletter style is so old fashioned. Let me use one of my new and cool faces, like C h i c k e n ! It's easier to read than this silly font!

Love,
Sonny Boy

# The Art of Readability

Readability and legibility are two elements of printed text that typographers strive to maximize. **Readability** refers to whether an *extended* amount of text—such as an article, book, or annual report—is easy to read. **Legibility** (discussed in the next chapter) refers to whether a *short burst of text*— such as a headline, catalog listing, or stop sign—is instantly recognizable.

## What makes a typeface readable?

There are several factors that determine whether text is readable. Most typefaces are either high or low on the readability scale simply due to the way they are designed. But a typesetter or designer can make any readable face unreadable, and conversely she can improve the readability of any face. It is your job to be conscious of both.

What makes a typeface intrinsically readable? Mainly it is a matter of a moderation of features, an invisibility. That is, whenever a feature of a typeface becomes noticeable, that face becomes slightly less readable. If a typeface has a very distinctive lowercase g, so distinctive that it makes you stop and say, "wow, look at that g," then it is lower on the readability scale.

Any part of the type that calls attention to itself—thick strokes, very thin strokes, a strong contrast between the thick and thin strokes of a letterform, very tall and narrow forms, short and squatty forms, slanted characters, fancy serifs, swashes, or other extreme features—lowers the readability of the face because then you notice the letterforms rather than the message.

# The most readable

The typefaces that make the most readable text are the classic oldstyle serif faces (remember those from Chapter 1?), either remakes of the original ones or new faces built on oldstyle characteristics. These typefaces were originally designed for long documents, since that's all there was in print at that time (late fifteenth to early seventeenth century). There were no brochures, advertising, business cards, packaging, freeway signs—there were only books. Big books. (In fact, it was Aldus Manutius, whose face made it into the 20th century on software packaging, who printed the first portable books in 1495.)

## Other factors

Besides the distinguishing features of the typeface, there are other factors that can make text more or less readable, as described on the following pages. Once you are conscious of these factors, you can work with them to make even the least readable face more usable.

This is Belwe Light. Does your eye trip over the lowercase g or v or y? If your eye stumbles over the look of the type, it's not good for extended text.

This is Bernhard Modern, a very beautiful face, but too distinctive for extended readability. Great for brochures or other places where there is not an extended amount of text.

*These faces have strong, noticeable features which make them quite distinctive. They are thus attractive for many uses, but there is too much distraction built into the faces to make them easy to read in extended text.*

This is Minion Regular, a lovely font that was created specifically for lots of reading.

This is Garamond Pro Regular, also a lovely font that was created specifically for lots of reading.

*Oldstyle typefaces have moderate features: there is moderation in the serifs, in the weight of the strokes, in the contrast between the thick and thin parts of the strokes, and in the x-height. I'll bet you can hardly tell these typefaces apart, right? It is this moderation, this lack of calling attention to the typeface itself, that makes oldstyles "invisible," which is ideal for communicating without an attitude.*

. . . . . . . . . . . . . . . . . . . . . . . . . . . . . . . . . . . . . . . . . . . .

# Serif vs. sans serif

There are arguments about exactly why, but extensive studies do show that today in our society it is easier to read an extended amount of text when it is set in a serif typeface. Perhaps it is the serifs themselves that lead the eye from one character to the next, linking the letters into words. Perhaps it is the subtle thick-thin contrast in the strokes, which most sans serifs do not have. Perhaps it is the moderate ratio of x-height to cap height (the body of the letter in relation to the height of the capital letters or the ascenders), since sans serif letterforms tend to have larger x-heights.

Whatever the reason may be, accept the truth of it and use the knowledge in your typography.

*Garamond Regular, 11-point type*

She had not gone much farther before she came in sight of the house of the March Hare; she thought it must be the right house, because the chimneys were shaped like ears and the roof was thatched with fur. It was so large a house, that she did not like to go nearer till she had nibbled some more of the left-hand bit of mushroom, and raised herself to about two feet high: even then she walked up towards it rather timidly, saying to herself, "Suppose it should be raving mad after all! I almost wish I'd gone to see the Hatter instead!"

Lewis Carroll, *Alice in Wonderland*

*Formata Regular, 10-point type*

She had not gone much farther before she came in sight of the house of the March Hare; she thought it must be the right house, because the chimneys were shaped like ears and the roof was thatched with fur. It was so large a house, that she did not like to go nearer till she had nibbled some more of the left-hand bit of mushroom, and raised herself to about two feet high: even then she walked up towards it rather timidly, saying to herself, "Suppose it should be raving mad after all! I almost wish I'd gone to see the Hatter instead!"

Lewis Carroll, *Alice in Wonderland*

*Which of these feels easier to read? If you really want to use sans serif in your body copy, shorten the line length, add a little extra linespace, and use a smaller size type than for a serif.*

# Caps vs. lowercase

Text set in all capital letters (all caps) is more difficult to read. We don't read letter by letter—we read in phrases. When you see a word, you don't sound it out letter by letter, do you? No, you glance at the word, recognize it, and move on. A significant factor in our recognition of whole words at a time is the *shape* of the word. But when words are set in all caps, every word has a rectangular shape and we have to go back to reading the letters.

Now, although all caps are definitely more difficult to read, especially when there is a lot of text, sometimes you *want* the rectangular shapes of all caps. If that is an appropriate solution for your piece, do it freely. Just keep in mind that you are making a choice to exchange better readability for a design choice — sometimes it's worth it.

Temper this decision with the purpose of your piece. If you really need strength in readability, as in extended text (or in the case of all caps, more than ten words), or if you want people to be able to browse quickly as in catalog headings, a parts list, the phone book, a list of names and addresses, headlines, a table of contents, then don't use all caps!

Momma   Poppa   Sister   Brother
MOMMA   POPPA   SISTER   BROTHER

*You can see how the shapes of the words in lowercase are so different from each other, helping us identify them. In all caps, all words have the same shape.*

*Is this word Momma, Poppa, Sister, or Brother?*

*Does this shape represent the word cat, dog, or garbage?*

# Letter spacing and word spacing

Again, since we read in phrases, uneven letter and word spacing disturbs our natural reading pattern; our eyes have to make constant adjustments between words. Spacing that is consistently too close or too far apart also disturbs our reading. There is no perfect rule that will fix the spacing for every typeface and every project—you must simply learn to see more clearly and then *trust your eyes*. If it looks like the words are too close together, they are. If it looks like the letters are too far apart, they are. Once you recognize appropriate and inappropriate spacing, you have the responsibility to learn exactly how your particular software controls the letter and word spacing. Ha! Read that manual.

Many script faces have connecting letters that need slightly *tighter* letter spacing so their letters will actually connect, but they also often need *extra* word spacing because the tails of the letters bump into the spaces between the words. Again, I cannot emphasize enough that you need to know how to control the spacing in your page layout application! (Most word processors do not have features to fine-tune the letter spacing.)

You are guaranteed to get poor word spacing if you justify text in a narrow column, so don't do it. How do you know if it's too narrow? See the next page.

*It isn't what I do, but how I do it.*

*It isn't what I say, but how I say it.*

*And how I look when I do it and say it.*

Mae West

*So which one of the lines above is too tight? Which one has too much word space? Which one looks okay? See how good you are at this already? Trust your eyes.*

# Line length and justification

If a line is too long, we have trouble finding the beginning of the next line. If a line is too short, it breaks up those phrases we recognize. If you try to justify your type on a short line, you will get awkward word spacing and rivers. So how do you know what's a decent line length?

There are several rules of thumb to determine this measure. Some people suggest no more than nine to ten words on a line as a maximum, or no more than 2.5 times the alphabet, which is 65 characters. The rule I find easiest to remember for an optimum line length (the minimum line length for justifying) is this:

> Double the point size of your type, and use a line length no
> longer than that in picas.

Say what? Well, let's say your type size is 9 point—your line length should be 18 picas. If your type is 24 point, your line length should be 48 picas.

All you have to remember is that there are 6 picas in one inch: thus 18 picas is 3 inches; 48 picas is 8 inches. (Did you read page 18 about points and picas?)

*Don't justify any text if your line length is shorter than this minimum!* If you're using a classic, readable oldstyle and you really want it justified but you find that the word spacing varies too much even on this line length, make the line a few picas longer and perhaps add a tiny bit more linespace.

Figure out your optimum line length and then analyze your typeface. Shorten the line length of *non-justified* text for these reasons:

- If the typeface has a very large x-height or a very small x-height.
- If the typeface is a sans serif.
- If you are reversing the type out of a background or solid color.
- If the typeface is script, decorative, or at least rather odd.
- If you are presenting type where it is difficult to read, such as on a presentation slide or on a web page.

# Linespacing (leading)

Linespacing is, obviously, the space between the lines. You have total control over how much space appears. Linespacing that is too tight decreases readability because it makes it difficult for the reader to separate the individual words and phrases, and it also makes it more difficult for the reader's eyes to find the beginning of the next line.

You will generally need to **increase linespacing** for these reasons:

- If the line length is longer than average.
- If the typeface has a large x-height, as most sans serifs do.
- If you are reversing the type out of a background or solid color.

You can **decrease linespacing** on an average line length if your typeface has a very small x-height since the small x-height creates more space between the lines naturally. But often when using a distinctive typeface with a small x-height, it is nice to reinforce that airy, open feeling by actually adding more linespace. See Chapter 15 on linespacing for more details and specific examples.

My way is and always has been to obey no one and no thing except that reasoning which seemed best to me at the moment when I made my decision. Never judge past action by present morality.

Socrates

*The paragraph above is set with the default linespacing (leading) value. Notice it seems a little tight between the lines. Typeface is Formata Light.*

My way is and always has been to obey no one and no thing except that reasoning which seemed best to me at the moment when I made my decision. Never judge past action by present morality.

Socrates

*Just adding one point of space in the paragraph above helped to open up the text so it is more pleasant to read. Sometimes all you need to add is half a point; sometimes you'll need to add several extra points.*

. . . . . . . . . . . . . . . . . . . . . . . . . . . . . . . . . . . . . . . . . . . . . . .

# Reverse type
# and light or heavy weights

White type on a dark background (reverse) appears to be smaller than black type on a white background. Compensate for this by using a slightly heavier typeface and slightly larger point size. If you have a Pro version of an OpenType font (see Chapter 30), use the caption weight, which is a little heavier.

| Which type appears smaller? | Which type appears smaller? |

**Never reverse a typeface that has delicate features —
very thin lines and tiny little serifs will clog up with ink and disappear.
Doesn't this look awful?**

The same guideline applies for text that is dropped out of a graphic image. I know it looks great on the screen, but when ink hits absorbent paper, all kinds of havoc is wreaked upon unsuspecting delicate type. Don't let your work look foolish by ignoring the realities of the reproduction process.

**Extra bold type** and extra light type are also less readable than a regular weight face. If you use them, be sure to compensate—you may need extra letterspace, extra linespace, a bit larger or smaller point size. Your eyes will tell you what is necessary.

On **web pages,** avoid colored text on a dark background. If you must, enlarge the size of the type a wee bit, and don't use bold or italic except in small doses.

# Italic or script

*Italics and scripts are more difficult to read in general because of their tight spacing, their curves and slants, their approximations to handwritten letterforms. Don't ever use them for extended text or no one will read your work. Maximize their readability:*

- *Pay close attention to their letter and word spacing.*
- *Increase their linespacing if necessary.*
- *Make the line length shorter than average.*
- *Don't reverse them unless they are set in a relatively large size.*

*Do you find this section less readable, even in this small amount of copy? Yes, these things are true—I am not just making them up.*

· · · · · · · · · · · · · · · · · · · · · · · · · · · · · · · · · · · · · · ·

# Moderation is the key

I'm sure you see the pattern by now—moderation in every facet of typography is the key to eminent readability. Now, this does not mean that you have to be dull and boring and moderate at all times! It just means that you need to be conscious and make conscious choices.

- ❧ Perhaps you want to use a very distinctive face in a brochure. If the face itself is not intrinsically readable, then make up for it in other areas of readability—an appropriate line length and word spacing, avoid all caps, etc. Make sure that all other text is eminently readable, and then you can get away with areas of fancy type.

- ❧ If you want to use a sans serif in body copy, use a shorter line length and a little extra space between the lines.

- ❧ If you want to reverse text, make it a bit bolder and larger, and don't use a fine-featured typeface that has tiny little serifs or thin lines that will disappear.

- ❧ Save extra bold and italic and extra light for accents.

- ❧ If your typeface has an extra-large x-height, use more linespacing. If it has very tall ascenders, you can use less linespacing.

- ❧ If you're setting a book, manual, magazine, or other lengthy text, including a lot of text on a web page, use the most readable face in all its moderation. Save the distinctive faces for chapter titles, headlines, subheads, poetry, etc.

**THROUGH TYPOGRAPHIC MEANS,** the designer now **preSents, in O**ne image, both the message and the pictorial idea.

Sometimes, this "playing" with type has resulted in the loss of a certain amount of legibility. Researchers consider this a deplorable **state of af-fairs, but on the other** hand, the excitement created by a novel image sometimes more than compensates

for the slight *DIFFICULTY* in readabil- ity.

Herb Lubalin

# The Art of Legibility

**Readability,** as discussed in the previous chapter, refers to whether an extended amount of text—such as an article, book, or annual report—is easy to read. **Legibility** refers to whether a short burst of text—such as a headline, catalog listing, or stop sign—is instantly recognizable.

There have been extensive studies on type to determine which factors influence different aspects of reading, such as reading speed, retention of information, recognition of letterforms, etc. Interestingly, these studies show that in our culture and in our era, serif typefaces are easier to read when there is a lot of text, but sans serif letterforms are more instantly recognizable when there is a small amount of text. Sans serif characters tend to be direct and clear, with no serifs to add unnecessary tidbits to the shapes. When we read a large body of text, however, those same serifs help to guide us along the lines.

We don't read letter by letter; we see the entire word or the phrase and it goes straight to our brains. When text is less than perfectly legible, we have to take extra time to read it. Sometimes this is only a split second, sometimes it's a more significant struggle, but it can make a big difference in whether the information is absorbed or tossed aside.

Text needs to be most legible (as opposed to readable) in situations where people are scanning pages, reading signs, or skimming through catalogs or lists—wherever they need to instantly recognize words without having to spend extra seconds to read them. For instance, in a newsletter, the headlines should just pop right off the page into the reader's brain. In a parts list, the reader should be able to slide down the page, absorbing the names of parts. In a table of contents, a reader should be able to scan the contents. Street signs, "Warning," "Danger," and all freeway signs should be instantly recognizable.

# What are you saying?

Always be conscious of the words themselves. Some words, such as "Sale," can probably be set in just about anything and people will get it. But if you have an unusual name, don't set it on your business card in a typeface that is difficult to read! If words are long or foreign and extremely important, be especially careful to choose a typeface with great legibility.

**Sale**   **Sale**   SALE   S a l e

*Waliciewskie Design*   WALICIEWSKIE DESIGN

# What makes type legible?

Not all sans serif typefaces are eminently legible. One of the keys to legibility is the clarity of the letterforms, or how easy it is to distinguish one character from another. For instance, the typeface Hobo eliminates the descenders (see below); this is useful in certain applications, but it is not what we are accustomed to and thus this feature decreases its legibility.

**I don't make jokes. I just watch the government and report the facts.**
**Will Rogers**

*Legibility depends on the instant recognition of letterforms.*
*When characters have odd shapes, we don't recognize them instantly.*

. . . . . . . . . . . . . . . . . . . . . . . . . . . . . . . . . . . . . . . . . . . . . . . . . .

# Large or small x-height

An exceptionally large x-height decreases legibility. Some faces have such large x-heights that an "n" is hardly different from an "h."

And a very small x-height also decreases legibility. The body of the character is disproportionate to the cap height, and our eyes find this to be distracting —besides the fact that the letters appear too small.

**I dote on his very absence.**    William Shakespeare

*Notice there is not much difference between the "n" and the "h," nor between the "i" and the "l" in "William." Typeface is Antique Olive Roman.*

Hercules himself could not beat out his brains, for he had none.  William Shakespeare

*Although this typeface is pretty and very distinctive, it is not the most legible. Typeface is Bernhard Modern.*

· · · · · · · · · · · · · · · · · · · · · · · · · · · · · · · · · · · · · · · · · · · · · · · · · ·

# Weight and proportion

❧ **Extra-heavy or extra-thin weights are less legible. A good solid bold, however, as long as it is not extra-heavy or condensed, can enhance legibility by giving a substantial contrast to the rest of the text. For instance, headlines are great in bold because the contrast of their weight attracts attention against the background of gray, readable text. But how do you like reading even this short paragraph in an extra-bold face (Antique Olive Compact)?**

❧ A monospaced font (such as Courier) creates inconsistent letter and word spacing, which makes it less legible (and less readable) because our eyes have to keep adjusting to the differences in spacing. Some faces are so poorly spaced that words can be misread at a glance.

❧ Using the computer to compress the typeface distorts its proportions and makes it less legible. If you want a compressed face, buy a specially designed font. See Chapter 12 for details and more examples on this topic.

# All caps or
# mixing caps and lowercase

❧ Mixing Lowercase And Caps In The Same Sentence Makes Type Less Legible *And* Less Readable. Your Eyes And Brain Have To Figure Out What's Going On Because We Are Not Accustomed To Reading This Way. This Is Called Title Case And Is Meant For Titles, Not Sentences or Captions.

## Killing time takes practice. Karen Elizabeth Gordon

*This typeface, Peignot, is interesting but not particularly legibile. Or readable. It mixes caps and lowercase in the middle of words, confusing our pea brains.*

❧ WORDS SET IN ALL CAPS ARE THE LEAST LEGIBLE OF ALL, NO MATTER WHICH TYPEFACE YOU USE. MANY PEOPLE THINK IF YOU SET TYPE IN ALL CAPS IT IS BIGGER AND THEREFORE EASIER TO READ. Wrong. We recognize words by their shapes as well as by their letters. Set in all caps, all words have the same shape. Have you heard this before?

| INDEPENDENCE AVE. | Independence Ave. |
| CONSTITUTION AVE. | Constitution Ave. |
| MASSACHUSETTS AVE. | Massachusetts Ave. |

*In Washington, D.C., the streets have long names. The street signs are set in all caps, squished to fit into the standard green shape. Consequently, you must get very close to a sign to tell what it says. If the street names were in upper– and lowercase, you would be able to tell Independence Avenue from Constitution Avenue long before you could actually read the letters.*

. . . . . . . . . . . . . . . . . . . . . . . . . . . . . . . . . . . . . . . . . . . . .

# The most legible type

To make your text the most legible, use:

- A plain sans serif with an average x-height.
- A regular or medium weight (sometimes bold when appropriate).
- Lowercase letters (plus capitals where they belong).
- Not condensed or expanded or oblique (slanted).
- A little extra letter spacing in small point sizes (below 10 point); less letter spacing in large sizes (above 14 or 18 point).

*Which of the following type samples is the most legibile?*

**1. Few forgive without a fuss.**    Hobo

*2. Few forgive without a fuss.*    *Dear Sarah*

**3. Few forgive without a fuss.**    **Antique Olive Bold**

4. FEW FORGIVE WITHOUT A FUSS.    THE WALL

**5. Few forgive without a fuss.**    **Peignot**

6. Few forgive without a fuss.    Formata

7. Few forgive without a fuss.    Bernhard Regular

*Answer: 6, Formata.*
*Can you see why?*

. . . . . . . . . . . . . . . . . . . . . . . . . . . . . . . . . . . . . . . . . . . . . . . . . . . .

# Temper the rules with choice!

Now, please remember that these guidelines do not mean you should never use certain typefaces or formatting! It just means you must look carefully at your typeface and make a conscious choice—if your piece requires a high level of legibility, watch for the danger signs. If your job is one that people can take a tiny bit longer to absorb or if the words are not unusual, then feel free to play with features that are not at the top of the legibility list. Use that beautiful face with the tall ascenders and small x-height for a sign, or that lovely, graceful script for a special title, or that extra-bold face for web page headlines. People can *read* it, of course. Know the guidelines, be conscious of your typeface and your purpose of communication, and make clear decisions based on knowledge.

And don't forget Herb Lubalin's theory, as presented on page 42. Lighten up and smile.

I OFTEN QUOTE MYSELF.

IT ADDS SPICE TO MY CONVERSATION.

GEORGE BERNARD SHAW

# Quotation Marks— or not?

If you are choosing to read this book, you are probably already conscious of the difference between typewriter quote marks (" ") and true quotation marks (" "), often called "curly quotes" or "smart quotes." But let's make sure you are also using single and double prime marks where appropriate, and leaving the ditto marks in their place.

## First, a review of quotation marks and apostrophes

Most software has a checkbox called something like smart quotes, true quotes, typographer's quotes, or a similar phrase, like one of these:

☑ "Smart quotes"

☑ Use Typographer's Quotes

Replace
☑ "Straight quotes' with "smart quotes"

If you check that box, the software will automatically insert true quotation marks when you type the " key on the keyboard. You will also get a true apostrophe when you type the ' key on the keyboard, as displayed below:

"No, don't do this."      "Yes, isn't this better?"

But be careful—if you trust the computer to always put the correct mark in the correct place, you will find people snickering at your work. For instance, when the automatic feature is on you will get quotation marks where you need inch and foot marks, like so: Bridge Clearance 12'6". Or when you have a quotation mark that appears right after a dash—"like this"—the quote mark goes the wrong way!

You need to know the key combinations to type the correct single and double quotes, both opening and closing, for those times when your software doesn't do it correctly. See the charts in Appendix C.

# Don't embarrass yourself

Follow these basic rules so your work doesn't look dumb:

- Quotation marks at the beginning of a word or sentence are *opening quote marks* and curl *toward* the text (" ).

    Quotation marks at the end of a word or sentence are *closing quote marks* and curl *toward* the text (").

    These are often called "sixes and nines" because the opening marks are shaped like sixes and the closing marks are shaped like nines.

- An apostrophe belongs where a letter is missing, as in **cookies 'n' cream** or **rock 'n' roll.**

    Notice your computer automatically inserts a ***backwards*** apostrophe at the beginning of a word! For instance, your computer will do this: **cookies 'n' cream.** This is WRONG! And dumb!

    Know the keyboard shortcut to insert the correct mark:

    | To type this: | Mac | Windows |
    |---|---|---|
    | opening single quote ' | Option Shift ] | Alt 0145 |

- The word **it's** with an apostrophe means *it is* or *it has*. **Always.** Really and truly **always.**

    The word **its** *without* an apostrophe is the possessive form of the word, as in *hers, his, theirs,* or *its.* Notice none of those possessive words contains an apostrophe. *Don't put an apostrophe in **its** unless you mean **it is** or **it has!***

- When talking about decades, such as **in the '90s,** there is an apostrophe where the other numbers are missing.

    Make sure you set an apostrophe and not an opening single quote! The phrase should not look like this: **in the '90s,** which is what you will get if you let the computer type it for you.

    Also notice there is no apostrophe before the s (not **in the '90's**) because generally you are referring to a plural number of years, not a possessive number.

# Single and double prime marks

Another problem with letting your computer automatically type the quotation marks for you is that you end up with quotation marks and apostrophes when you really need inch and foot marks.

Wrong: **Ryan stands 6'2" tall.**    Right: **Ryan stands 6′ 2″ tall.**

Now, you might think that you should be typing those ugly typewriter apostrophes and quotation marks for inch and foot marks. Wrong, dear. In excellent typography, feet and inches are represented by single and double *prime marks,* which are at a slight angle, as shown below.

These are typewriter quote marks: **" '**

These are double and single prime marks: ″ ′

If you have the Symbol font on your computer (which you probably do), you can use the prime marks in it:

| **To type this:** | | **Mac** | **Windows** |
|---|---|---|---|
| single prime mark | ′ | Option 4 | Alt 0162 |
| double prime | ″ | Option Comma | Alt 0178 |

However, it's very possible that the prime marks in the Symbol font do not match the weight of your characters. Until every font has prime marks built in, you might often have to use the italic version of your typewriter apostrophes or quotations marks, as shown below.

Using the Symbol font might look inconsistent: **Kiki stands 5′ 8″ tall.**

Use italic typewriter marks: **Kiki stands 5′ 8″ tall.**

Technically, prime marks are not meant specifically as inch and foot marks, but as markers of divisions of equal parts. For instance, you would also use the single prime mark to show the minutes or degrees of an angle or a turn, as in 12° 8′ (read 12 degrees and 8 minutes).

· · · · · · · · · · · · · · · · · · · · · · · · · · · · · · · · · · · · · · · · · · · · · · · · · · · · · ·

# When to hang it

Punctuation should always be hung when type is set aside from the main body of text or when set large, as in a quotation, pull quote, headline, poster, etc. If the type is set flush right, the periods or commas at the ends of the lines should also be hung if they interrupt the right edge of the type. (Except in very fine typography, punctuation in body text is usually not hung because of the trouble it takes and because the interruption in the line is not as significant when the type is small.)

"I'm laughing
at the thought
of you laughing,
and that's how laughing
never stops in this world."
**Zorba the Greek**

"I'm laughing
at the thought
of you laughing,
and that's how laughing
never stops in this world."
**Zorba the Greek**

*I'm sure you agree that both of these pieces of type need the punctuation hung.*

"I'm laughing
at the thought
of you laughing,
and that's how laughing
never stops in this world."
**Zorba the Greek**

"I'm laughing
at the thought
of you laughing,
and that's how laughing
never stops in this world."
**Zorba the Greek**

*Oooh, look at those nice clean edges. The strength of that edge gives strength to the page. Typeface is Bailey Sans Bold.*

# Optical alignment

The point of hanging the punctuation is to keep a strong left or right edge. Often this means aligning the edge with a stem (vertical stroke) rather than with a bar (horizontal stroke), as in the letter "T." Align the second line of type with whatever is the strongest edge of the initial character you see—remember, your eye is always right! *If it doesn't look aligned, it isn't.* You might have to align with the bottom point of the capital "V," or just inside the outside curve of an "O." Whichever part of the letter is the closest or most obvious visual connection, align with it. This is called "optical alignment" because you are not aligning by a ruler, but by your eye.

**"You believe easily
that which you
hope for earnestly."**

Terence

*Even though the top edge of the letter "Y" is aligned with the second line of type, it still appears to be indented. That's because our eyes see the vertical stem of the "Y," rather than the top angle, much more closely related to the "t." Typeface is Today Sans Medium.*

**"You believe easily
that which you
hope for earnestly."**

Terence

*Above, the stem of the "Y" is visually aligned with the "t." This is an optical alignment rather than a measured alignment.*

. . . . . . . . . . . . . . . . . . . . . . . . . . . . . . . . . . . . . . . . . . . . . .

# Just how do you hang it?

At first, hanging the punctuation might seem like a silly task. But as your typographic consciousness is raised, I guarantee you will also begin to see it as a sign of professional type. There are several methods of doing this, depending on the project and the software.

## Software features

InDesign can hang the punctuation with the click of a button. From the Type menu, choose the "Story" palette. Put a check in the box, "Optical Margin Alignment." Enter the point size of your type. This will hang punctuation even in the middle of a paragraph, when it's flush left, flush right, or justified. This applies to the entire *story* and can slow down the redraw and composition, so only use it when necessary.

QuarkXPress can hang the punctuation of left-aligned type. For repeated instances of hanging indents, use the "Formats" command in the Style menu. For a single instance you can use the key command for "Indent Here," which is Command/Control \ (backslash).

## Use an indent

If you have to hang the punctuation by hand, one of the easiest ways is to use an indent, as shown below. This works when the quote is a paragraph on its own and is flush left. If you use this setup regularly in your publication, make a style sheet for it.

**"It's as large as life
and twice as natural,"
said Alice.**

*Set your indents so the first line marker is flush left, and the left indent marker is aligned along the stem of the first letter.*

## Reverse the punctuation

This next trick is kind of a kludge (which means a dorky solution), but it works: select the punctuation and paste it in front of (or at the end of, if flush right) each of the other lines. Select the punctuation you have pasted in and then choose the "reverse" style from your font formatting menu to make the characters invisible. (In a word processing application, you might not have the option to make type reverse; perhaps you can color it white.)

The reason I suggest you paste the punctuation instead of simply typing it is that very often when type is set fairly large (above 14 point), you need to reduce the size of the punctuation so it doesn't appear unnecessarily important. By pasting the punctuation, you ensure that all your reverse spaces are the same size, even if you changed the type sizes.

**"Run mad
as often as
you choose,
but do not
faint."**

Jane Austen
in *Mansfield Park*

**A.** *The punctuation
needs to hang.*

**"Run mad as."
often as you."
choose,"
but do not."
faint."**

Jane Austen.,"
in *Mansfield Park*.

**B.** *Paste in copies
of the punctuation.*

**"Run mad as
often as you
choose,
but do not
faint."**

Jane Austen
in *Mansfield Park*

**C.** *Reverse the
punctuation you
don't need.*

## Use hard spaces

A "hard space" is an empty space that is different from the regular space that you type with the Spacebar. A hard space doesn't "break" like a regular word space does—a non-breaking, hard space connects two words as if they were one word. For instance, to prevent the name "Ms. Scarlett" from breaking into "Ms." at the end of one line and "Scarlett" at the beginning of the next line, you would type a hard space between "Ms." and "Scarlett," and then the phrase "Ms. Scarlett" would never break into two words

You can indent on the left or right with hard (non-breaking) spaces, if your software allows it (try it and see). Almost all applications can set a standard hard, non-breaking space in place of the regular blank space, and some, like Adobe InDesign, can set em, en, and thin spaces (see the charts in Appendix C). Use these blank spaces to indent lines of type so you have a strong flush alignment. If the space you set is too large, select that blank space and reduce the size of it.

**"I knew who I was when I woke
up this morning, but I must have
changed several times since
then," said Alice.**

**"I knew who I was when I woke
up this morning, but I must have
changed several times since then,"
said Alice.**

*In this example, I typed an en space in front of the first word of every line (except the first one) to align them with the first letter in the paragraph.*

· · · · · · · · · · · · · · · · · · · · · · · · · · · · · · · · · · · · · · · · · · · · · · · · · ·

## Kern outside the text block or box

If for some reason you must do it by hand, try this in your page layout application: Insert a hard space *in front of* the first quotation mark. Then kern until the quotation mark hangs outside the text block or box. In QuarkXPress, the mark may seem to disappear, but it will print just fine.

"But look, the morn, in russet
mantle clad, walks o'er the dew
of yon high eastward hill."
**Horatio**

*Notice the quotation mark is
hanging outside of the text block.*

| To type this: | Mac in general | Windows |
|---|---|---|
| non-breaking space | Option Spacebar | Alt 0160 |
| | **Mac InDesign** | **Windows InDesign** |
| | Command Option X | Control Alt X |

In InDesign, you can also select the space and use the contextual menu (right-click; on a Mac, Control-click); choose "Insert White Space," then "Nonbreaking Space."

# Punctuation Style

All of us now circumvent the professional typesetter and create beautiful publications on our own desktops. We've heard all about the typesetting standards of setting one space after periods, and how to access em dashes and en dashes and true quotation marks and apostrophes. Although most of us know how to *create* these alternate characters, there still seems to be considerable confusion over *when* to use them. The punctuation in your publication affects the professional appearance of your work just as powerfully as the characters themselves. (It's interesting that when the "rules" of design are broken it is called "creative," but when the established rules of punctuation are broken it is called "uneducated." Creative punctuation is not a well-accepted idea.)

So following are some guidelines to help give your desktop-designed work a more professional edge. If you have other questions, read *The Chicago Manual of Style*, William Strunk's wonderful little book, *The Elements of Style*, or check the back of your dictionary—most dictionaries include a basic manual of style.

It is often the very small details that set mediocre work apart from outstanding work. To push a publication to the professional edge, make sure you carry your style all the way through, even to such mundane principles as punctuation.

# Quotation Marks

Of course you are using proper quotation marks (" ") and not typewriter marks
("). American standards decree that periods and commas be placed inside
quotation marks, *always.* Like it or not, that's the way it is in America; some
other countries do it differently.*

> **"Oh Bear," said Christopher Robin, "How I do love you."**
> **"So do I," said Pooh.**

**Colons** and **semicolons** are always placed *outside* the quotation marks, and they
are both followed by one space.

> **This is how to pronounce "forte":  fort.**
>
> **Most people mispronounce "victuals"; it is properly
> pronounced "vittles."**

**Exclamation points** and **question marks** follow logic: If the mark belongs to the
quoted matter, it goes inside. Otherwise it is set outside.

> **She said, "I love to crack crawdads!"**
>
> **Did she say, "I love to crack crawdads"?**
>
> **She asked me, "Don't you love to crack crawdads?"**
>
> **My son warned me, "Mom, I met a girl who loves to crack crawdads"!**

*\*Note: The delightful book that you may have seen called **Eats, Shoots and Leaves**
is from Britain where they use quotation marks differently (essentially, their rule
is similar to our rule, above, about exclamation points and question marks). In
the American version, the publishers did not adjust the book for American usage;
consequently, every quotation mark in that book is **WRONG** according to our
standards. It's rather odd that a book bitterly complaining that people don't
follow the correct standards did not standardize the book for its market here.*

# Parentheses

If the text inside the parentheses is just an aside within or at the end of a sentence (like this one), then the punctuation goes after and *outside* the closing parenthesis.

If the text inside the parentheses is a complete sentence that starts with a capital letter and ends with a period (or other final mark), then the punctuation belongs *inside* the parentheses. (This is an example.)

There are no extra spaces surrounding parentheses, other than the normal word space before and after. There is no extra space between the closing parenthesis and any punctuation that might follow.

**Meet me under the magnolia at twilight (without the wig), and we will waddle down the trail together.**

*Notice the comma is directly after the parenthesis, and there is just the regular word space after the comma.*

Also see Chapter 7 for information on when you might need to shift the baseline position (up or down) of the parentheses.

. . . . . . . . . . . . . . . . . . . . . . . . . . . . . . . . . . . . . . . . . . . . . .

# Apostrophes

In contractions and informal writing, the apostrophe belongs where the letter is missing. Remember that simple principle and you will never go wrong. I repeat myself on this because it is so important; the misuse of the apostrophe is rampant and really annoying.

In case you missed it: One of the two most common mistakes in typography is with the word **and** between words such as **Mom 'n' Pop** or **peaches 'n' cream.** Set the apostrophe where the letters are missing! If a letter or number is missing at the beginning of a word, *don't turn the apostrophe around so it looks like an opening single quote.* It *should* be an apostrophe.

To know where the apostrophe belongs in **possessive words,** turn the phrase around. The apostrophe belongs *after* the word in the turned phrase. For instance, "all the horses oats." Is it all the oats that belong to the *horse* (which would then be *horse's oats*) or all the oats that belong to the *horses* (which would then be *horses' oats*)? Notice the apostrophe is set *after* the word you used in the turned-around phrase.

## Its or It's

The other most prevalent mistake is the word **its.** Do you put an apostrophe in *hers,* or *his,* or *theirs,* or *yours?* No. The word **its,** when possessive, is in the same category as hers, his, and yours—*there is no apostrophe!* **It's** with an apostrophe always, always, always reads **it is** (or *it has*). **Always.**

# Ellipsis

The ellipsis character (the three dots: …) is used to indicate where text has been omitted from the original material. There is a character on your keyboard for this.

| To type this: | Mac | Windows |
|---|---|---|
| ellipsis … | Option Semicolon | Alt 1033 |

But this character is too tight for professional typographic standards. You can type a space between periods, but then it might break at the end of a line and you would have one or two periods at the beginning of the next line. Preferably, type a thin or en space before and after each period in an ellipsis (see the chart at the end of the book). If you can't type thin or en spaces kern the three periods open. If you have an ellipsis at the end of a sentence, type a period after the ellipsis.

Wrong: **It's so...silly.**          Right: **It's so . . . silly.**

# Type style

The style of the punctuation should match the style of the word it follows. For instance, if a word followed by a comma is **bold,** then the comma itself should also be bold. You may have a semicolon following *italic words;* the semicolon should be italic. Follow the same principle for any style change.

Parentheses, though, do not pick up the style unless everything within the parentheses is the same style. That is, if all the text in the parentheses is italic, then the parentheses are both italic. But if only the last word is italic, the parentheses are set in the regular style of the rest of the text. The same goes for bold or any other style change. Like so:

She's willing (and able) and she'll be ready in a while.

She's willing (and I do believe she's ***able***), but not ready.

She's willing *(but not able)* and will be ready in a while.

Don't worry if you think it looks a little odd to have a big fat bold period or comma in the middle of your **paragraph,** like so. This is one of those things you get used to and then the wrong way begins to look glaringly wrong. It's like knowing that the pronunciation of the word **forte** (as in "Pickle-making is my forte") is really "fort," not "fortay." The word "fortay" means "loud, forcefully," as in music notation. At first it sounds wrong to say "fort," and you must have conviction to pronounce it properly among others who assume you are wrong, since most people pronounce it incorrectly. But once you accept that "fort" is the correct pronunciation, "fortay" is wrong (unless you choose to use a dictionary that has succumbed to popular pronunciation rather than correctness, which is what happens to our language). (Oh well.)

· · · · · · · · · · · · · · · · · · · · · · · · · · · · · · · · · · · · · · · · · · · · · · · · · · · · · · · · ·

# Em dashes

Text within parentheses is like whispering; text within commas is an average statement; text within em dashes is more emphatic. The example below illustrates this concept.

Use em dashes to set off a phrase that has a lot of commas in it—like this, and thus, and so—to avoid confusing the reader.

Or mark an abrupt change in thought or sentence structure—I learned this yesterday—with an em dash.

Em dashes are set with no space before or after the dash. This bothers many people, though, because the dash tends to bump into the letters. So add a tiny bit of space on either side by kerning (see Chapter 14 on Kerning). But if you insert an entire word space before and after the dash, you exacerbate the interruption in the flow of text.

The origins of printing are almost as obscure as the origins of writing, and for much the same reason — its inventors never used their new medium to record the process.
Sean Morrison

The origins of printing are almost as obscure as the origins of writing, and for much the same reason—its inventors never used their new medium to record the process.
Sean Morrison

*When there is a space on either side of an em dash, it creates a disturbing gap in the text and calls too much attention to itself. Typeface is Memphis Light.*

*Kern a little bit of space on either side of the em dash, if necessary, just enough so it doesn't bump into the letters.*

| To type this: | Mac | Windows |
|---|---|---|
| em dash — | Option Shift Hyphen | Alt 0151 |

. . . . . . . . . . . . . . . . . . . . . . . . . . . . . . . . . . . . . . . . . . . . . . . .

# En dashes

The most common use of an en dash is to indicate a duration. Read the sentence; if you substitute the word "to" for the dash, then the proper mark is an en dash. Actually, in a real sentence I would spell out the word "to," but you will often find occasions outside of sentences where an en dash is the appropriate mark.

> **All children ages 3–10 are welcome to attend
> the crawdad party from 6–8 p.m. every Monday
> from September–November.**

En dashes are commonly used with a little extra space on either side, especially when indicating a duration. Either add a little space with your kerning function, or insert a thin space on either side—*do not* type a whole word space with the Spacebar on either end of the en dash.

Also use an en dash instead of a hyphen in a compound adjective when one of the items is two words or a hyphenated word.

> **She took the New York–London plane to be at the opening
> of the post–Vietnam War presentation.**

> **The Internet cafe was filled with the over–sixty-five crowd.**

| To type this: | Mac | Windows |
| --- | --- | --- |
| en dash – | Option Hyphen | Alt 0150 |

. . . . . . . . . . . . . . . . . . . . . . . . . . . . . . . . . . . . . . . . . . . . . . . . . .

# Hyphens

Just because you know how to use em and en dashes, don't ignore hyphens! Em and en dashes do not replace hyphens—they simply replace *the incorrect uses of the hyphen.* If you are breaking a word at the end of a line, or if you are using a compound adjective as in "blue-green eyes," of course type a hyphen!

The following situation is difficult to describe, so I am going to illustrate it instead. When you have something like this:

**Martha was both a first-place and second-place winner in the gravedigging contest.**

"First-place" and "second-place" are adjectives composed of two words, making them "compound." You probably want to combine those compound adjectives into something like this:

**Martha was both a first- and second-place winner in the gravedigging contest.**

Does it bug you that the word "first" has a hyphen after it? Well, too bad because that is the correct way to set the text. The hyphen indicates that this word is also connected with the rest of the adjective. Once you understand and accept the correctness of it, you can have a little uppity attitude when you see others set it wrong. Gently teach them.

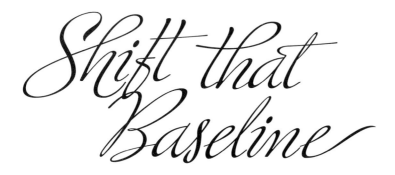

# Shift that Baseline

Ahhh, so you have surely by now read *The Mac is not a typewriter* or *The PC is not a typewriter,* as well as the previous chapters in this book, and you have been diligently typing one space after periods, using real apostrophes and quotation marks, putting the apostrophes in the right places, and creating true fractions. Right? Now that you're feeling sassy, it's time to move on to a more sophisticated matter: baseline shift.

First, let's clarify the term **baseline.** The baseline is the invisible line upon which all the characters sit, as shown below. Some characters, such as j, p, g, and y, have strokes that hang below the baseline; these strokes are called the "descenders." The term "baseline shift" refers to moving characters up or down in relation to that baseline.

## I have a frog in my pocket, darling.

*The grey line indicates the baseline of the text. Most characters are designed to sit directly on the baseline; descenders hang below.*

Once you are familiar with the baseline shift technique, you will find uses for it more often than you might think!

· · · · · · · · · · · · · · · · · · · · · · · · · · · · · · · · · · · · · · · · · · · · ·

# Parentheses and hyphens

I'll bet it drives you nuts that the hyphens in phone numbers seem set too low. And the parentheses around the area codes bump into the numbers, which probably makes you crazy. You see, parentheses and hyphens are designed to be used with lowercase letters because that is where they appear most of the time. So when these characters are used with all caps or numbers, they appear to be low in relation to the taller size of the caps or numbers. But, thank goodness, this can be fixed.

Below, I shifted the hyphen and the parentheses up a little higher until they appeared to be centered—doesn't it look much better, more consistent, in better balance? There is no scientific formula for the exact placement—*your eye is the judge.* If it looks centered, it is. If it looks too low, it is. If it looks too high, it is. Listen to your eyes.

(707) 123-4567                    (707) 123-4567

*The parentheses bump into the tops of the numbers, but hang below the bottoms. Also notice how low the hyphen sits.*

*To make parentheses and hyphens appear to be in the correct position when you're working with caps or lining numbers, raise them up a little.*

**A.** The Cul-de-Sac reopens (dinner only)

**B.** THE CUL-DE-SAC REOPENS (DINNER ONLY)

**C.** THE CUL-DE-SAC REOPENS (DINNER ONLY)

*Parentheses and hyphens are designed for lowercase letters, since that is where they are used most often (**A**). If you use all caps (**B**), the hyphens and parentheses are too low. Raise them higher off the baseline to make them appear centered (**C**).*

. . . . . . . . . . . . . . . . . . . . . . . . . . . . . . . . . . . . . . . . . . . . . .

# Dingbats as bullets

Another occasion to take advantage of the baseline shift feature is when using dingbats or ornaments. Suppose you have a list of items and you really want to use a fancy dingbat from the Zapf Dingbats or Wingdings font, instead of using the boring ol' round bullet (or—heaven forbid—a hyphen). But the dingbat character is usually too big. When you reduce its size, though, the dingbat is too low because the character is still sitting on the baseline. So select the character and shift it higher up above the baseline.

**Pick any three adjectives that describe yourself:**

- Ruffatory
- Doaffie
- Byblow
- Regnant
- Backgone
- Illy-willy
- Fustian
- Dorty
- Fuzzled

**A.** *Choose a dingbat instead of the dumb ol' bullet or hyphen.*

**Pick any three adjectives that describe yourself:**

✣ Ruffatory
➜ Doaffie
✳ Byblow
❤ Regnant
❖ Backgone
❑ Illy-willy
❀ Fustian
✺ Dorty
▼ Fuzzled

**B.** *You have lots of dingbats to choose from, but they are usually too big. (Choose one dingbat.)*

**Pick any three adjectives that describe yourself:**

▾ Ruffatory
▾ Doaffie
▾ Byblow
▾ Regnant
▾ Backgone
▾ Illy-willy
▾ Fustian
▾ Dorty
▾ Fuzzled

**C.** *You can decrease the point size of the bullet, but then it sits too low.*

**Pick any three adjectives that describe yourself:**

▾ Ruffatory
▾ Doaffie
▾ Byblow
▾ Regnant
▾ Backgone
▾ Illy-willy
▾ Fustian
▾ Dorty
▾ Fuzzled

**D.** *Raise the small dingbat higher off the baseline.*

. . . . . . . . . . . . . . . . . . . . . . . . . . . . . . . . . . . . . . . . . . . . . . . . .

# Initial caps

You can also create a quick initial cap with baseline shift. Change the size and font and perhaps color of the first letter. If it disrupts the line spacing, select the entire paragraph and apply a fixed amount of leading (just type in a number—don't use "auto"; see Chapter 15). Then select the first letter and apply the baseline shift downward—making sure the baseline of the letter aligns on one of the baselines of the paragraph! (See Chapter 24 for lots of suggestions for initial caps.)

The important thing about your lot in life is whether you use it for building or parking.

*In this paragraph, I selected the "T" and changed its typeface and size. I used the technique in Chapter 5 (hard space and kerning) to hang the "T" so it aligned with the rest of the text. I used the baseline shift feature to drop the bottom of the "T" down to the second line. I kerned the "h" in toward the "T."*

*Typeface is Bernhard Modern with the cap T in Scarlet.*

# Decorative words

You can also create interesting special effects with words, as shown below. Some of the letters have been shifted up, then kerned into the caps. The "W" has been shifted down slightly. The word "That" has been shifted up and kerned close, also.

*This arrangement was created with baseline shifts and kerning.*
*Typeface is Cocktail Shaker.*

. . . . . . . . . . . . . . . . . . . . . . . . . . . . . . . . . . . . . . . . . . . . .

# Corrections

Sometimes, especially in decorative type or logos, the characters are not exactly where you want them. So use your baseline shift to adjust their positions. Remember one of the Rules of Life: You are never stuck with anything. Get busy. Get creative.

**ZUMA'S**

i n t e r n e t   c @ f e

**ZUMA'S**

i n t e r n e t   c @ f e

*This is the way the text set as I simply typed it. I wanted the apostrophe lower and the Z to come down a bit to balance the word.*

*That's better, and that was easy.*

*Typefaces are Las Bonitas Bold and Schmelvetica.*

· · · · · · · · · · · · · · · · · · · · · · · · · · · · · · · · · · · · · · · · · · · · · · · ·

# How do you do it?

To baseline shift, check your manual. All page layout applications can shift the baseline, as well as many word processors. The *amount* of baseline shift is determined by your preferences, which you can change. Here are a couple of keyboard shortcuts for Adobe InDesign and QuarkXPress.

First select the character(s). Then:

**✶ Mac InDesign:**

    to move up       Shift Option ↑ (UpArrow)
    to move down   Shift Option ↓ (DownArrow)
Add the Command key to increase by 5 times the increment set in your preferences.

**✶ Windows InDesign:**

    to move up       Shift Alt ↑ (UpArrow)
    to move down   Shift Alt ↓ (DownArrow)
Add the Control key to increase by 5 times the increment set in your preferences.

**✶ Mac QuarkXPress:**

    to move up       Command Option Shift +
    to move down   Command Option Shift -
(Use the + and - from the keyboard, not the numeric keypad).

**✶ Windows QuarkXPress:**

    to move up       Control Alt Shift )
    to move down   Control Alt Shift (

# Expert Type

In which we look at OpenType, true-drawn small caps, compressed and expanded characters, as well as ligatures and oldstyle figures (numbers).

We also explore expert sets and discuss display type.

I would 'twere bedtime, Hal, and all well.

Falstaff

What I love most about the recent revolution in electronic design and communication is the explosion in the awareness of typography. People who, ten years ago, didn't know there was more than one typeface in the world now scrutinize menus and advertisements and posters, wondering what font is on the page.

It also never ceases to amaze me how quickly we become inured to the magic, how quickly we find that what we have isn't enough, how quickly we want more and better and bigger. It's hard to imagine that we could want more than the standard set of 256 characters in a typical font, which is many more than we had on typewriters. But we do, and that's just the way it is. And that's why several of the major font vendors created **expert sets,** which are additions to basic font sets designed for when we get to that point of wanting more and better, such as oldstyle figures, true small caps, fractions, swashes, display versions, superior and inferior characters, and extra ligatures.

And that's one reason why Adobe and Microsoft jointly created **OpenType,** which takes advantage of the double-byte of the latest operating systems, both Mac and Windows, to let us have fonts that can contain more than 65,000 glyphs (variations of characters).

In this chapter I'll explain what OpenType and expert set fonts are and why you might want to use them. In the following chapters I elaborate on when and why to use each of the expert typographic features.

· · · · · · · · · · · · · · · · · · · · · · · · · · · · · · · · · · · · · · · · · · · · · · · · · · ·

# What's in an OpenType or expert set font?

This chapter is an introduction to what you might find in OpenType or expert set fonts. The following chapters elaborate on the various typographic features, such as those listed below, that you'll find in these special fonts.

## Small Caps

Almost any program can turn selected lowercase letters into SMALL CAPS, where a capital is still a capital and the other letters become capital letters about the height of lowercase letters. The problem, though, is that the computer simply reduces the size of the existing capital letters. This creates a proportion distortion between the cap and the small cap, where the capital letter appears much heavier than the corresponding smaller capitals, as shown on page 90. In many OpenType and expert set fonts, the small caps are not just small capitals, but are letterforms that have been totally redesigned to visually match the large cap in the same point size. See Chapter 9.

## Oldstyle figures

Regular numerals (figures), such as 45,872, appear too large when set within body text. Numerals used to be designed like lowercase letters, with ascenders and descenders, like so: 45,872. Many OpenType fonts and expert sets include these oldstyle figures, which blend smoothly with the body copy. Oldstyle figures are also particularly beautiful when set in extra-large sizes. Once you start using them it's hard to go back to the other characters. See Chapter 10.

## Display type or titling caps

Traditionally, small letterforms and large letterforms in a well-designed typeface differ not just in their height, but in their thick/thin stroke differences, the proportion of the x-height to the cap height of the character, the space between the letters, and the open space in the "counters" (the holes in letters like e, g, or c). But on the computer when you use a large point size, say 128 point, of a regular font, the computer just takes the 12 point size and enlarges it to 128 point. The letterforms start looking a little clunky.

Some expert fonts offer display type (which includes lowercase) or titling capitals. The characters in display typefaces have been specially designed for larger sizes, those above 24 point. The difference isn't readily noticeable at 24 point, but becomes quite significant on headline or poster-sized type. See Chapter 13. OpenType fonts sometimes include not only a display version of the typeface, but separately designed versions for captions and subheads. See page 84.

. . . . . . . . . . . . . . . . . . . . . . . . . . . . . . . . . . . . . . . . . .

## Ligatures

In addition to the standard ligatures *fi* and *fl* (Mac only) expert sets usually offer many more combinations, such as an Rp for rupees or &t for special effects in words like a&tion. See Chapter 11. OpenType fonts might include dozens of great ligatures; see page 85.

## Swash characters

The more elaborate expert sets offer alternate swash characters that can add a nice touch to your work. *Remember*, swash characters are like cheesecake—it's easy to overdose. And be sensible where you place them. The swash is meant to end a phrase or tuck under adjacent letters, not to create an unsightly gap. *See Chapter 23*. Swash characters are often built into the italic version of an OpenType font.

## Em dashes

Convention decrees that we set em dashes with no space on either side—like so. But those long dashes often bump right into the letters and have to be manually letterfit. Many people insist on using a space on either side of the em dash, which exacerbates the interruption in the reading and creates an even larger gap in the overall look of the type. Some expert sets contain a wonderful character that solves this problem—a ¾-em dash with a thin space built into both sides. You have to look for it, unfortunately.

## Ornaments

There are often pretty little ornaments (❦ ⎯ ❧  🙣  ～  ✿  🌼  🌸) in expert sets and OpenType fonts that offer elegant alternatives to dingbats. See Chapter 26.

## OpenType in particular

There is so much to tell you about OpenType fonts. Please see pages 84–86.

· · · · · · · · · · · · · · · · · · · · · · · · · · · · · · · · · · · · · · · · · · · · · · · · · ·

## The details are delightful

The subtle distinctions that OpenType and expert sets offer would have passed fairly unnoticed in the general public years ago. But the level of type sophistication has increased so dramatically across an incredible variety of professions, so the subtle distinctions in type are now being noticed and appreciated. Even though the changes are what some may call minor, the overall professional effect comes through clearly.

This life is but a Penelope's web, where we are always doing and undoing; a sea open to all winds, which sometime within, sometime without never cease to torment us; a weary journey through extreme heats and colds, over high mountains, steep rocks, and thievish deserts. And so we term it in weaving at this web, in rowing at this oar, in passing this miserable way.

A Discourse of Life and Death translated by Mary Sidney Herbert, 1592 original in French by Philipe de Mornay

*This is a simple example of the difference the specialty fonts in an expert set can make in a piece of type. To the left is plain ol' Times Roman, 12/14.5, justified.*

*T*HIS LIFE IS BUT A PENELOPE'S WEB, where we are always doing and undoing; a sea open to all winds, which sometime within, sometime without never cease to torment us; a weary journey through extreme heats and colds, over high mountains, steep rocks, and thievish deserts. *A*nd so we term it in weaving at this web, in rowing at this oar, in passing this miserable way.

A DISCOURSE OF LIFE AND DEATH
*translated by Mary Sidney Herbert & 1592*
original in French by Philipe de Mornay

*This is Brioso Pro Regular, 10.5/15, with small caps, display swash italic, regular swash italic, and oldstyle proportional numerals. The bylines use Brioso Pro Caption, also with small caps, an ornament, italic, and oldstyle numerals.*

# Expert set fonts

You can buy expert sets at most of the font web sites (see a partial list in Appendix B). Because a regular font can only hold up to 256 characters, an expert set is actually a collection of fonts in the same family. That is, in an expert package you will get the regular font, plus you might get a font that contains just the small caps, another that contains oldstyle figures, superscripts, and subscripts. And yet another for italic swash. A complete expert set package might contain up to thirty different fonts in the one family! Each font will show up in your font list separately (see pages 87–88).

An expert set font might be labeled "Expert," "OSF," "SC," "Small Caps," or some other descriptive term. Be sure to check the specifications and the samples for the font before you invest in it.

*This is the Adobe Caslon Expert family with all the individual fonts for the regular character set and each of the expert additions.*

Before you run out and buy a bunch of expert sets, carefully read about OpenType. OpenType is eventually going to replace expert sets. If you're using InDesign, skip expert sets and move right into OpenType. If you're using QuarkXPress, any version earlier than 7.0, you're stuck with expert sets.

. . . . . . . . . . . . . . . . . . . . . . . . . . . . . . . . . . . . . . . . . . . . . . . . .

# OpenType fonts

OpenType is a font format from Adobe and Microsoft. It's based on Unicode, which uses a double-byte encoding system. You don't need to know the technical points of it—all you need to know is that by using this encoding, a font can now contain more than 65,000 glyphs instead of the basic 256 we've been limited to all this time.

A **glyph** is an individual symbol for a character. For instance, the lowercase letter "z" is a character. But you might have a capital Z, a small cap z, a swash Z, and an accented Ź. Each of these is considered a glyph, even though they are all the same character.

An OpenType font can include **entire character sets** for true-drawn small caps, fractions, swashes, ligatures—all explained in the following chapters.

With the possibility of more than 65,000 glyphs in one font, it's also possible for one font to include **multiple language characters.** For instance, an Adobe OpenType Pro font typically includes Cyrillic characters for Russian and other Slavic languages, a full range of accented characters to support European languages such as Polish and Turkish, and even Greek characters. μ'αγαπάς;

OpenType fonts are **cross-platform** — you buy one font file and it works on Mac, Linux, Unix, and Windows platforms. This is a tremendous help when files are moving between one operating system and another.

An OpenType font might include several **optical size variations**. As explained in more detail on page 80, fonts really should be redesigned for different sizes, not just enlarged or reduced on the computer screen. An OpenType font might provide you with a redesigned version of the typeface specifically to be used in small sizes, called the **caption** font for 6- to 8-point text; a **regular** version for 9- to 13-point text; a **subhead** version for 14- to 24-point; and a **display** version for 25- to 72-point or larger. In the examples below, you can see the different weights and thick-thin proportions in each of the variations, depending on the point size at which it's designed to be used—smaller type needs to be a little heavier with a little more letterspacing; larger type needs thinner thins and less letterspacing.

Warnock Pro Caption, 18 point
Warnock Pro Regular, 18 point
Warnock Pro Subhead, 18 point
Warnock Pro Display, 18 point

## OpenType fonts are smart

When you use OpenType in an application that knows what to do with it, you'll find that OpenType fonts are "smart." That is, they automatically substitute characters that are more appropriate in particular typographic situations.

For instance, when you set type in all caps, OpenType adds the appropriate amount of baseline shift so characters such as hyphens and parenthesis fit better (see Chapter 7).

In a script face, glyphs might change depending on whether the character is at the beginning, in the middle, or at the end of a word. In a handwriting font, OpenType can automatically use different glyphs for the same characters so the set text more closely resembles handwriting.

❶ *This* **e** *is designed for use in the middle of a word. The connector on the left side usually attaches to the previous letter.*

❷ *This* **e***, without a connector, is great when* **e** *is the first letter of a word or directly after a capital letter to which it will not connect.*

❸ *This* **e** *is obviously perfect for the last letter.*

❹ *This* **e** *is great as the first character in a word that appears on its own line (so the swash won't bump into the previous word).*

❺ *Ministry Script also has a huge number of ligatures.*

The OpenType face used for the chapter openers in this book is Ministry Script from Umbrella (shown in the examples above), available at Veer.com. Flip through the chapters and take a look at the huge variety of glyphs, including ligatures, available in this font. Below is the font Zapfino, which is included with Mac OS X. The different ligatures and glyphs for the letter "f" appear automatically; you can see OpenType change its mind as you type. Notice also the lovely ligature for the "Th."

. . . . . . . . . . . . . . . . . . . . . . . . . . . . . . . . . . . . . . . . . . . . . . . . . . . .

**Adobe InDesign** makes using OpenType a breeze. Below you see my font menu
for an OpenType font called Warnock Pro. You can see the menu itself tells
me it's an OpenType font by the little "O" icon next to its name. Once I have
selected the optical size and style I want to use, I can use the Glyphs palette
(farther below) to select specific characters.

*InDesign's font menu is great.
It displays the font's format,
a sample of it, and organizes
the family very nicely.*

*The Glyphs palette displays
every character in a font.*

When you see a tiny triangle in the corner of a glyph's box, you know there are
alternate glyphs for that character. Click on the triangle to see the alternates,
as shown above. Double-click a glyph to make it appear on the page where the
insertion point is flashing or where text is selected.

# Small Caps

THERE ARE A NUMBER OF TECHNIQUES that designers and typographers use to make type more beautiful and pleasant—one technique is the use of small caps. Small caps are capital letters that are approximately the size of lowercase letters. Small caps are often used simply for their design effect, but they have several very practical uses in fine typography. Sometimes an article or chapter opening begins with the first line (or part of the first line) in small caps, as in this paragraph. This is a simple, elegant way to lead the reader into the text.

## Where to use small caps

If you set acronyms in regular all caps, their visual presence is unnecessarily overwhelming. One standard and practical way to use small caps is in acronyms such as FBI, NRC, CBS, or SIMM.

Traditionally, "A.M." and "P.M." are set with small caps. If you were taught to type on a typewriter (or if you were taught by someone who learned on a typewriter), you were probably told to set these abbreviations in all caps because there were no small caps on typewriters. But now that you have the capability, you can and should set them properly.

Harriet, an FBI agent, turned on CNN to get the dirt
on the CIA before going to bed at 9:30 P.M.

Harriet, an FBI agent, turned on CNN to get the dirt
on the CIA before going to bed at 9:30 P.M.

*The capital letters in the middle of the sentence call too much attention to themselves. Notice how the small caps blend in with the text. The capital letters for P.M. are much too large—the abbreviation is not that important.*

. . . . . . . . . . . . . . . . . . . . . . . . . . . . . . . . . . . . . . . . . . . . .

# Readability and legibility of small caps

Pull quotes and captions are sometimes set with small caps, but keep in mind that small caps are no easier to read than all caps. Since every word in all caps is a rectangle, our eyes have to resort to reading letter by letter. This does not mean you should *never* use all caps or small caps—just be aware of this limitation and use them when you can justify the loss in readability and legibility. The more text there is in all caps or small caps, the less likely it is that people will read it.

TO LIVE CONTENT WITH SMALL MEANS; TO SEEK ELEGANCE RATHER THAN LUXURY, AND REFINEMENT RATHER THAN FASHION; TO BE WORTHY, NOT RESPECTABLE, AND WEALTHY, NOT RICH; TO STUDY HARD, THINK QUIETLY, TALK GENTLY, AND ACT FRANKLY; TO LISTEN TO STARS AND BIRDS, TO BABES AND SAGES, WITH OPEN HEART; TO BEAR ALL CHEERFULLY, DO ALL BRAVELY, AWAIT OCCASIONS, HURRY NEVER. ❧ IN A WORD, TO LET THE SPIRITUAL, UNBIDDEN AND UNCONSCIOUS, GROW UP THROUGH THE COMMON. ❧ THIS IS TO BE MY SYMPHONY.

WILLIAM HENRY CHANNING

*Do you find that, even though the text is interesting, you have to struggle to stay with it? Small caps are no easier to read than all caps.*

# Oldstyle Figures

In typography, numbers (or numerals) are called **figures.** Most typefaces use plain old regular numerals, or figures. These regular numerals (also called "lining figures") are similar to all caps in that they appear to be too large when set within body text. But figures used to be designed like lowercase letters, with ascenders and descenders, which blend smoothly and beautifully with body copy. These "oldstyle figures" are also particularly beautiful when set in large sizes. Once you start using them it's hard to go back to the regular lining number.

*Notice how large and clunky these figures appear:*

Dear John, please call me at 438-9762 at 3:00 to discuss marriage.
Or write to me at Route 916, zip code 87508.

*Notice how beautifully these figures blend into the text:*

Dear John, please call me at 438-9762 at 3:00 to discuss marriage.
Or write to me at Route 916, zip code 87508.

. . . . . . . . . . . . . . . . . . . . . . . . . . . . . . . . . . . . . . . . . . . . . . . . . . . . . . . .

# Setting ligatures

You can always set the fi and fl ligatures in any application in any font on the Mac. If you want other ligatures or if you use a PC, you will have to invest in an OpenType font or an expert font set. To set these ligatures in any Mac font:

fi    Option Shift 5

fl    Option Shift 6

InDesign: Select the text, then from the little menu in the Character palette, choose "Ligatures." Use this in the appropriate style sheets. Ligatures will not cause spell-check problems and will separate when kerned.

QuarkXPress: From the QuarkXPress menu, choose "Preferences," then "Character." Check the "Ligatures" box. Unfortunately, this applies to the entire document regardless of point size or font, which makes it almost useless for professional typography. (The "Break Above" amount is a kerning value so if you letterspace your type beyond that amount, the ligature will automatically separate back into the two characters.)

# The dotless i

Generally, ligatures are not used in display type (type in large sizes, above 24-point). If you have a problem with the hook of the "f" bumping into the dot of the "i," try using the dotless i character: ı (type Option Shift B, Mac only). Or use the Glyphs palette in InDesign to find and insert the dotless i.

## Flying fish found in pocket!

*Notice the problem in the "fi" combination.*

## Flying fish found in pocket!

*The dotless i solves this problem so neatly.*

This dotless i character also comes in handy any other time the dot gets in the way, as might happen if you use italic swash caps.

## *Victor Hugo    Victor Hugo*

*Oooh, doesn't that dot bumping into the V bother you? Now you can fix it.*

# Condensed and Extended Type

Type families often have more members than the basic Regular, Italic, Bold, and Bold Italic—a larger family might have Condensed, Bold Condensed, Extra Condensed, Extended, Black Extended, etc. Some typefaces are single-member families and are designed specifically as one very condensed or very extended look.

**Condensed** type is type that looks like it has been *compressed,* or squished, horizontally, but not vertically. **Extended** type seems to have been *expanded,* or stretched horizontally. You can use condensed or extended type for practical typographic solutions or simply for playful effects.

This is Eurostile Plain, a great face.

This is Eurostile Condensed, another great face.

This is Eurostile Extended, also great.

*Condensed faces often have a "tall," elegant look.*

*Extended faces usually appear squatty, yet appealing.*
*They often have a high-tech, assertive look.*

· · · · · · · · · · · · · · · · · · · · · · · · · · · · · · · · · · · · · · · · · · · ·

# Condensed text faces

Condensed text faces are handy when space is at a premium. You've probably noticed that some typefaces take up a lot more room than others. Compare the space occupied by the copy set in the two faces below, Garamond and Times. Times was created for the *London Times* specifically to save space yet still be eminently readable. You can tell even in this small sample that a large body of text in Times would fill significantly less space than the same size type in Garamond, even though Times appears to be larger (because of its x-height; see page 17 for details about the x-height).

They have a wonderful therapeutic effect upon me, these catastrophes which I proofread . . . . When the world blows up and the final edition has gone to press the proofreaders will quietly gather up all commas, semicolons, hyphens, asterisks, brackets, parentheses, periods, exclamation marks, etc., and put them in a little box over the editorial chair. *Comme ça tout est régle.*

Henry Miller, *Tropic of Cancer*

They have a wonderful therapeutic effect upon me, these catastrophes which I proofread . . . . When the world blows up and the final edition has gone to press the proofreaders will quietly gather up all commas, semicolons, hyphens, asterisks, brackets, parentheses, periods, exclamation marks, etc., and put them in a little box over the editorial chair. *Comme ça tout est régle.*

Henry Miller, *Tropic of Cancer*

*The face on the left is Garamond; on the right is Times. Both are set 9/12.*

## Computer-drawn vs. true-drawn

You can compress and expand type through most software applications with the click of a button. This is okay for an occasional emergency, but the computer distorts the type by simply squishing it. If you need a compressed face so you can, for instance, get more words into your newsletter, please don't let the computer squish the type—invest in a "true-drawn" condensed face. True-drawn faces have been redesigned with different proportions, stroke thicknesses, counter spaces, and other fine features so as to retain the integrity of the typeface and maintain readability. Below are examples of what the computer does to the letterforms as opposed to what the designer does.

# Franklin Gothic, condensed
# Franklin Gothic Condensed

*In the first example, the computer simply squished the letterforms. The second example is a redesigned face. Notice the differences in the weight, the thin/thick strokes, the counters (spaces inside the letters), the letter spacing, the height of the lowercase letters in relation to the caps, the terminals of the "e" and "s" where open space has been designed into the condensed version, and other subtle differences between the computerized version and the redesigned face.*

As for me, I am tormented with an everlasting itch for things remote. I love to sail forbidden seas and land on barbarous coasts.

Herman Melville, *Moby Dick*

*A well-designed condensed text face maintains maximum readability within the compressed proportions. This is an example of a true-drawn Garamond text face called Garamond Light Condensed.*

## Break the rules

Occasionally you may want to create some dynamic display of type and you need a condensed or extended version, but it doesn't exist or it isn't enough. It's okay to break the rules, but break them with gusto! Make it look like you *meant* to distort the type. If it's not obvious, the sophisticated reader (of whom there are more and more) will think you just didn't know what you were doing. Don't be a wimp!

*If you're going to distort type, then do it! Do it so it's obvious—don't pretend you're not distorting it!*

*Typefaces are Dulcimer (script), Eurostile Bold Extended Two, and Bad Copy.*

Display type refers to type that is large, that is on display, as opposed to body text, which is what you read in paragraphs at smaller point sizes (9 to 12 point). Some people might refer to headlines as display type, but generally it refers to type at least 24 points or above. Decorative typefaces are also called display faces, because you would typically use them only at large sizes for special occasions.

Now, the definitions above are generic definitions. There is also an actual classification of type design called "display type." These faces have been specifically redesigned for larger sizes.

Long ago, when type was carved by hand out of metal, the designer changed subtle features as the sizes got larger: the thin strokes got thinner, the serifs were more delicate, the counters (the space inside the letters) were different, the places where parts of the letters joined were thinner, the letter spacing was tighter, sometimes the ratio of x-height to cap height was different.

The computer, however, makes no distinction between sizes of type. It takes one size, say 12 point, and makes it larger or smaller as you wish. Thus when you use 6-point type, it is simply half of 12-point. This means the strokes are half as heavy, the space between the characters is half as much, etc. When you set 36-point type, it is simply three times as large as 12—the thin strokes are three times thicker, there is more space between the characters, etc. This creates a heavy, clunky look at large sizes. The solution to this problem is to use a specially designed display face.

## Display vs. text

It is easy to see the differences in the two faces below. Both are the typeface Warnock Pro, an OpenType font, but the word on the left is set with Warnock Pro Regular; the word on the right is set with Warnock Pro Regular Display (all examples are set in 80-point type). The instant impression, even if a person is typographically illiterate, is that the display face is finer and more elegant, less chunky and clunky. That's because the letterforms and spacing attributes in the display face have been designed specifically for larger type sizes—they have not been simply enlarged.

pox
*Warnock Pro Regular*

pox
*Warnock Pro Regular Display*

*pox*
*Warnock Pro Italic*

*pox*
*Warnock Pro Italic Display*

PAR
*Warnock Pro Regular*
*with small caps*

PAR
*Warnock Pro Regular Display*
*with small caps*

*Take notice of exactly what makes these faces different, which details create the more elegant look of the display face. Look carefully at the serifs, the thick/thin contrasts in the strokes, the places where the parts of the characters join together, the letter spacing, the crispness of the terminals. Which would you choose to use in a billboard or large poster?*

*Display faces usually come in families of at least Regular, Italic, Bold, and Bold Italic, all designed for large type sizes.*

# Display type and body text

If you have a display face, don't use it in body text! If the computer takes a display face and reduces it, those delicate thins and serifs will be so weak in the smaller size that they'll fall apart when it prints. Remember, if the face was designed at 36-point and you print it at 9, the computer will just reduce everything in the entire face to a quarter of the original. Even if it prints well because you use a high-quality press, it will be less readable than the regular font at the smaller size.

Several of Adobe's OpenType fonts include optical size variations to make it possible to use a font designed for the size of type you are setting. "Opticals" include variations for captions (6–8 point), regular type (9–13 point), subheads (14–24 point) and display type (25–72 point). See Chapter 8.

*Below is Brioso Pro Regular, an OpenType font from Adobe set at 65-point. It's not really meant for large sizes—it looks rather heavy.*

# Serendipity

But Brioso Regular is *meant* for body text. It holds up quite well at this size you are reading right now. Even at 9-point, the strokes are even and full, and the proportions are ideally suited for readable text.

*Below is Brioso Pro Display, set at 65-point. The features of this font are more delicately designed than the regular Brioso face so it presents a more elegant presence on the page at the larger size.*

# Serendipity

But Brioso Pro Display is not as readable or graceful at this small, 9-point size you are reading right now. The proportion of the x-height is too large, the thins are too thin, the letter spacing is too tight, the delicate features are lost or wimpy.

you
can do
a good ad
without
good
typography,
but you can't
do a
great ad
without
good
typography.

hERB LuBALiN

# Spacing

In which we discuss
the importance of
and uses for
pair kerning,
auto kerning,
range kerning,
track kerning,
manual kerning,
word spacing,
and letter spacing,
as well as
linespacing (leading)
and paragraph spacing.

**The truth is**

that typography is an ART
in which Violent Revolutions can scarcely,
in the nature of things,
hope to be successful.
A type of Revolutionary Novelty
may be extremely beautiful in itself;
but for the creatures of habit that we are,
its very Novelty
tends to make it illegiblE.

**Aldous Huxley**
Typography for the Twentieth-Century Reader

In page layout applications, such as Adobe InDesign, QuarkXPress, or Adobe PageMaker, you have an incredible amount of control over the spacing between letters, words, and lines. But to take advantage of this control, you must know what the features refer to. Later in this section I address the space between lines (linespacing, or leading) and the space between paragraphs. This chapter focuses on manipulating the space between the letters: kerning, pair kerning, auto kerning, manual kerning, range kerning, tracking, and letter spacing.

## Kerning

Kerning is the process of adjusting the space between individual letters; it is a fine-tuning process. The desirable end result is visually consistent letter spacing because consistent spacing strengthens the readability of the text. Whether that means you increase space between tight letters or decrease space between loose letters, the spacing must be consistent. You don't want the reader's eye to stumble over awkward letterfitting. To a discerning eye, your kerning is symbolic of your attitude and experience toward type.

Canteloupe *This word is not kerned at all. The letters are loose, quite separate from each other.*

Canteloupe *This word has been kerned so the letters fit snugly and consistently together without being overly tight.*

· · · · · · · · · · · · · · · · · · · · · · · · · · · · · · · · · · · · · · · · · · · · · · ·

## Kerning metal type

Until the 1970s, type was set in metal. Some machines set entire lines of type on metal slugs, but many machines followed the older style of using individual pieces. Regardless of the particular method, every character had its own separate metal space. If each letter is on its own piece of lead, then the letters can only get so close to each other—it's simply not physically possible to move them closer without taking a knife and shearing off some of the lead, thereby making that character useless for further typesetting. In lines of metal type, you couldn't even do that much. In those days, designers had to cut apart the proof sheets of type and move the printed letters around to adjust their spacing, then glue them down. If you look at an old magazine, you can instantly tell it's old, right? One of the visual clues that tells you it's old is the loose letter spacing, looser than you are accustomed to reading now that type is being set electronically.

## Letter spacing

Letter spacing is not really kerning, but refers to a general and arbitrary adjustment of the space between characters in a large piece of text, whereas kerning is a form of individual letter spacing. You might want to add more letter space to open the look of a typeface, or to create a dramatic headline that stretches across the page. You might want to decrease the letter spacing of a script face so the connectors reach the following letters. Notice the very open (too open) letter spacing of this paragraph. It's rather annoying in this case, isn't it?

Whew. This is better. The letter spacing values that any good page layout application applies to a typeface are based on the values the designer built into the font. These are explained on the following pages.

Word processing applications generally don't use the kerning pairs (see the next page) to fit the letterforms together nicely. This is the biggest reason why you can always glance at a printed page from a word processer and instantly tell it came from a word processor and not a page layout application.

· · · · · · · · · · · · · · · · · · · · · · · · · · · · · · · · · · · · · · · · · · · · · · · · · · · · ·

## Kerning pairs

Most well-made fonts have "kerning pairs" built into them. That is, as designers create fonts, they build in tighter spacing between certain *pairs* of letters that are known to cause inconsistent gaps, such as Ta, To, Yo, we, and many others. Not all fonts have kerning pairs built in, and some have poorly adjusted pairs. Some fonts have 200–300 kerning pairs, others have over a thousand. Just because a font has an extraordinary number of kerning pairs does not mean it's better. In fact, when there are many thousands of pairs it can take longer to display the text on the screen, and it will also take longer to print.

## Auto kerning

Page layout applications usually have a checkbox that allows you to tell your program to automatically take advantage of the kerning pairs, if you are using a font that contains them. In most programs you can also specify a point size above which the kerning pairs are automatically used. It's neither necessary nor desirable to auto kern small sizes of type (less than about 7 or 8 point) because when type is set small it should actually have *more* space between characters, not less.

Adobe InDesign utilizes two methods of auto kerning. **Metrics kerning,** the default method, uses the font's built-in kerning pairs which are built into the font metrics. **Optical kerning** takes the shapes of each letter pair into consideration and adds or removes space based on the letter shapes. Optical kerning is the best option when you are combining characters from different typefaces (as in the third example, below), which obviously wouldn't have kerning pairs built in because they come from two different fonts.

# Well Told Vermin Take woe

*InDesign unkerned type*

# Well Told Vermin Take woe

*InDesign metrics kerning*

# Well Told Vermin Take woe

*InDesign optical kerning*

*You can clearly see the difference in the letterspacing—look at the ends of the lines. In type this large you will always have to do some manual kerning because auto kerning is just a start.*

## Manual kerning

Kerning is a totally visual skill. The computer does the best it can with what it has to work with, but the end result, especially for larger type sizes, depends entirely on your eyes and your judgment. So even if your application has used auto pair-kerning, you must usually kern the larger type manually, selecting the space between two letters and adjusting it to match the visual space between the others.

Every page layout application and many illustration programs have keyboard shortcuts for kerning type on the screen. Sometimes you must insert a numeric value into a dialog box to add or remove the space, and some applications use both methods. Whatever it is, find out and use it.

*When you kern manually, you must either select the two letters you wish to kern between, or click to set the insertion point between the two (depending on your software).*

## Range kerning

Sometimes you start the fine-tuning process by selecting a "range" of text—a group of consecutive letters—and applying kerning values. This method, called range kerning, adds or removes *the same amount of space between every pair of letters,* regardless of their natural letterfit. If you range kern large type (14-point or over), you will probably need to finish the process by manually kerning certain combinations.

*When you select a range of text (as shown to the left) and apply a kerning value or use keyboard shortcuts to kern, you are taking out the same amount of space between every pair of letters. This is the first step in the process—you will still need to manually kern the characters for a perfect letterfit.*

. . . . . . . . . . . . . . . . . . . . . . . . . . . . . . . . . . . . . . . . . . . . . . . . . . . . . . . . . .

## Tracking

Tracking is a more complex issue, but only Adobe PageMaker uses true tracking. True tracking increases or reduces the letter spacing *according to the point size of the type.* If you use InDesign or QuarkXPress, you can skip the next three paragraphs.

Remember when we talked about display type, and how the original metal letters were redesigned for large and small sizes, and that the spacing values were different for large and small type? Small type requires extra letter spacing; large type, as in headlines, requires less letter spacing the larger it gets.

In PageMaker, if you choose Normal tracking for very *small* type, it *adds* letter space; if you choose Normal tracking for *large* type, PageMaker *subtracts* space. It takes all the built-in pair kerns into consideration as well, so you get as close to optimum letter spacing as possible before having to manually fine-tune.

You might want to add PageMaker's tracking to your headline style sheet so all your heads have a start on proper letter spacing (you may still need to manually kern pairs of letters). You might want to track all your caption style sheets that use very small type so they have the tiny bit of extra space they need. Because PageMaker's tracking is so thorough and complex, it's not a good idea to track large blocks of body copy—most body copy (9- to 12-point type) will not need tracking anyway. Reserve its power for large and small type.


The "tracking" in InDesign and QuarkXPress is simply *range kerning*—it adds or subtracts a fixed amount of space between all letters selected *regardless* of point size or kerning pairs already in use. The tracking value is *added* to any kern pairs or metrics/optical kerning that has been applied.

Find out exactly what your software does when you choose the tracking command. Whether it is true tracking or simply range kerning, understand what it does and use it when appropriate.

# Kerning definitions

These are brief definitions of the variety of terms related to kerning.

| What it is | What it means | When to use it |
|---|---|---|
| **Letter spacing** | Adding or decreasing the same amount of space between all the letters. Letter spacing is applied to a range of text; kerning is applied to individual pairs. | Usually used to change the spacing of a large amount of text to open the face or tighten it, depending on the natural characteristics of the typeface and its purpose on the page. |
| **Kerning** | General term for adjusting the space between letters. | Kern to create a visually consistent look. |
| **Pair kerning** | The special kerning built into certain combinations of letters when the typeface was designed. You can use special programs to add more kerning pairs to your fonts. | This is built into your font—don't worry about it. |
| **Auto kerning** | When an application is capable of automatically finding and using the pair kerns built into the font. | You can turn auto kerning on or off in your application. Leave it on. |
| **Metrics kerning** | An auto-kerning method that automatically uses the kern pairs built into the font. | When you are pretty confident that a typeface has kerning pairs built into it. |
| **Optical kerning** | An auto-kerning method that adjusts the fit of the letters depending on their shapes. | When combining characters from different fonts or using a typeface that does not include pair kerns. |
| **Manual kerning** | Adjusting the fit of two characters by "hand" (with the computer). | Use this for the final fine-tuning. |
| **Tracking (range kerning)** | Selecting a range of text and applying an overall kerning value to all the pairs of letters. | Use this to tighten a range of text in preparation for manual fine-tuning. |
| **Tracking (point-size specific)** | PageMaker only. Means by which the computer adjusts the letter spacing, depending on the point size of the type and the auto kern pairs. | Use this for large or very small type as a start for better letter spacing. For large type, you will still have to manually fine-tune the type. |

# Linespacing (leading)

Linespacing is the space between the lines of type. When type was set in metal (which wasn't that long ago), compositors would insert thin strips of lead (yes, the metal called lead) between the lines of metal characters, which is why the space is called "ledding," not "leeding." Leading is measured in *points*, just like type. The measuring system works like this:

*12-point type*
*+2 points of lead*
*=14 points of total*
*space, called leading*

You take the point size of your type, say **12** point.
You take a (metaphorical) thin strip of lead, say **2** points.
You add the **12** points of the type size
to the **2** points of lead, and you then say
that you have a leading value of **14** points.

This is written as **12/14** and is
pronounced "twelve on fourteen."

The phrase **12/14** used to mean that text should be set at 12 point
and the typesetter should then drop down 14 points
to the next baseline,
but now it simply means that there are 14 points of space
surrounding the line of type,
and various applications apply that space differently,
above and below the baseline.

Traditionally, an average leading is 20 percent
of the point size of the type.
Thus for 10-point type,
the average leading is 2 points,
added to the 10
which makes a 12-point leading value.
For 30-point type, an average leading is 6 points,
which makes a 36-point leading value.

So now if you look at a type specification that calls for 10/16, you instantly know there is a lot of space between the lines. If you see type that is set with the same number for the leading value as for the type size, such as 24/24, which is called "set solid," you know there is very little space between the lines.

· · · · · · · · · · · · · · · · · · · · · · · · · · · · · · · · · · · · · · · · · · · · · · · · · · · · · · ·

# Not-so-average linespacing

Although 20 percent of the point size of the type is an average linespace, there are many times when you need to change that. Here are details of several clear-cut cases for when you *must* adjust linespacing, other cases when you might *want* to, and a guideline for what to look at to determine the optimum linespacing for your text.

## Headlines

If a headline runs two or more lines, you will probably need to decrease the linespace. The average 20 percent is okay for body copy, around sizes 9 to 12, but above that it starts to become excessive, especially when you get into sizes such as 48 and 72. Also in big headlines, take note of whether you have descenders or not and where they fall. If there are no descenders, you really have to decrease the linespace.

### The orchestra played egregiously

### The orchestra played egregiously

*Notice, above, how much extra space there appears to be between the lines, especially since there are no descenders in the first line. You can take out quite a bit of space, as shown in the example on the right.*

*The setting on the left is 18 point type with an automatic leading value of 21.6, which is 20 percent.*

*The setting on the right is 18-point type with a leading value of 17 (which is actually what's called a "negative" amount of leading).*

*Typeface is Trade Gothic Bold No. Two.*

. . . . . . . . . . . . . . . . . . . . . . . . . . . . . . . . . . . . . . . . . . . . . . . . . .

## All caps

When text is all caps, there are no descenders that drop into the linespacing, but every one of the letters reaches up to the full height of the line. Because the words present such compact rectangles, you must be very conscious of the linespacing.

IN SMALLER SIZES, SUCH AS BODY TEXT (WHY WOULD YOU SET BODY TEXT  IN ALL CAPS?), BE CONSCIOUS OF THE CROWDED FEELING THAT SOMETIMES HAPPENS WITH ALL CAPS—BE LOOSE WITH LINESPACING.

THE PARAGRAPH ABOVE IS SET WITH AUTO LEADING, WHICH IS 120 PERCENT OF THE POINT SIZE OF THE TYPE. IN THIS PARAGRAPH I ADDED A FEW EXTRA POINTS OF LINESPACE TO LOOSEN AND LIGHTEN THE LOOK, WHICH MAKES IT EASIER TO READ (WHICH MEANS IT COMMUNICATES BETTER).

In large sizes, as in big headlines, the compact words in all caps emphasize the amount of space between the lines; it can look disproportionate. You will probably want to decrease the space between the lines so the entire headline looks like a compact package rather than separate lines.

**THE DAYS ARE ENDLESSLY DULL**      **THE DAYS ARE ENDLESSLY DULL**

*Eurostile Bold, 15/18*                *Eurostile Bold, 15/16*

*If, for some reason, you need to set headlines or other large type*
*in all caps, you will probably need to remove some of the linespace.*
*Without the descenders, the space appears to be excessive.*

. . . . . . . . . . . . . . . . . . . . . . . . . . . . . . . . . . . . . . . . . . . . . . . . . . . . . .

## Sans serif text

Sans serif typefaces tend to have large x-heights. These large x-heights fill the spaces between the lines, almost always necessitating extra linespacing. But look carefully at the face first! Do you think this paragraph could use a little extra leading? Yes? You're right. This paragraph is set with the standard extra 20 percent.

## Special effects

Sometimes you want to increase or decrease the linespacing dramatically for a special effect. Do it! Just make sure you do it with gusto. Don't just add a tiny bit more linespace—add a lot! Don't just make the text very tight between the lines—make it extraordinarily tight! *If you are going for the effect, then go all the way.* Don't be a wimp or it will simply look like a mistake.

## Watch for these features

| | |
|---|---|
| Large x-height: | Increase linespacing. |
| Small x-height: | Decrease linespacing. |
| Tall ascenders: | You can get away with less linespacing because the x-heights are relatively small, but you might want to actually add dramatic linespace to emphasize the tall ascenders. |
| Reverse type: | Along with increasing the point size by a point or two and increasing the weight a bit, you should probably also add a tiny bit more linespace. |
| Long lines: | If you must use long lines of text, add a tiny bit more linespace so the reader can find the beginning of the next line easily. |
| Wide letter spacing: | If the typeface is set with lots of letter spacing, add more linespace for balance. |

# Paragraph Spacing

The space between paragraphs is an important issue. Well, in the grand scheme of things I suppose it doesn't rank very high, but in typography it's important. If you space or indent your paragraphs poorly, your work betrays you as an amateur.

First of all, let's clear up one thing: either indent your paragraphs *or* put extra space between them. Don't do both. The purpose of an indent is to tell the reader that this is a new paragraph. A small indent does that just fine. A small amount of space between the paragraphs does the same. But if you use *both* an indent and extra spacing, it's like hitting your reader over the head with a baseball bat because you think he is too stupid to read the clues for a new paragraph. He is not stupid. Choose one method.

## Paragraph indents

So let's say you are going to indent your paragraphs. Are you going to indent them five spaces? One-half inch? No way. I know that's what your typing teacher taught you, and if you ever type across a page on a typewriter (if you can even find one) you usually need a five-space indent in proportion to the line length. But you are rarely setting lines that long on your computer, and besides, the standard typographic indent is one *em space.* An em space is a blank space as wide as the point size of the type; in 12-point type, an em space is 12 points; in 36-point type, it is 36 points. If you can set an indent with a measurement, set one em space. Otherwise fake it—an em space is more like two spaces than five.

Use your software to set the indent automatically. All word processors and page layout programs let you set a first-line indent; when you hit a Return, the text starts *at wherever you set the first-line indent.*

• • • • • • • • • • • • • • • • • • • • • • • • • • • • • • • • • • • • • • • • • • •

## First paragraphs are not indented

The purpose of an indent is to warn the reader that a new paragraph is about to begin, right? Well, if it's the *first* paragraph on the page or the first paragraph after a subhead, the reader does not need that clue—it's redundant. This is another one of those details where it might not look correct at first, but once you know it *is* correct and you apply it, other work will look foolish to you when the first paragraphs are indented.

## Space between the paragraphs

If you want space between the paragraphs, *don't hit double Returns!* That is, don't hit the Return or Enter key twice to make the space between the paragraphs. Learn to use your software to put an extra space after each paragraph, a space generally about half the amount of your linespace. If you hit two Returns you get a big gap, a gap that separates the very things that should be visually connected. The paragraphs on other pages in this book have a linespace (leading) value of 14 with 5.5 extra points of space after each paragraph.

But on this page I have hit double Returns. Aren't these huge spaces between paragraphs horrendous? It makes the work look so juvenile.

Again I must reinforce: learn to use your software. Every word processor and page layout application gives you control over the space between your paragraphs. Be smart. Look smart. Use it.

The alignment of your text plays a vital part in the look and the readability of your work. It's not the only factor—typeface, line length, style, size, linespacing, and case (caps or lowercase) also contribute. Type that is easy and pleasant to read encourages people to read what is written. Type that is not so readable can discourage a significant portion of the audience.

In short text, as in an advertisement or a package design, you can often get away with using a design feature that detracts from the readability but adds to the attractiveness and impact of the piece (such as extreme letter spacing, all caps with a justified alignment, or fringe type)—but this only works when you can justify that the *look* of the piece is more important than the accompanying loss of readability.

Passion without
reason is blind;
Reason without
passion is dead.

Will Durant
paraphrasing Spinoza

*A centered alignment
is very stable and secure
and tends to have
a more formal appearance.
It can be dull
because of this formality.*

Passion
without reason
is blind;
Reason
without passion
is dead.

Will Durant
paraphrasing Spinoza

*A strong flush right
or left alignment
has a clean edge
with an almost visible
line running along it.
The strength of this edge
adds strength to the design.*

· · · · · · · · · · · · · · · · · · · · · · · · · · · · · · · · · · · · · · · · · · · · · · · · · · · · · ·

# Left aligned

Speaking just in terms of alignment, text aligned on the left is the most readable. Left-aligned text uses the optimum word spacing and letter spacing that the designer built into the font, and the spacing is very consistent so you don't have to struggle through the words at all. And as you read, your eye can quickly find the beginning of the next line.

When you align text left, strive to keep the right, "ragged" side as smooth as possible, or in a slightly concave shape. Sometimes this necessitates forcing line breaks to fill in holes or to prevent long text strings from hanging beyond the rest of the lines. Below, the word *of* is hanging off the right edge, while in the line just below it there is clearly plenty of room to accommodate the word. Bump *of* down to the next line (see Chapter 22 on Line Breaks for details).

If you bump words down, be sure you do it as the last touch in your final layout. Otherwise when you edit the text, change the type size or column width, or alter the layout in any way, you will end up with tab spaces, empty spaces, or line breaks in the middle of your sentences. Fortunately, in a flush left alignment you can easily make type corrections and adjust lines, often without affecting the rest of the text at all.

1. I declare! Sometimes it seems to me that every time a new piece of machinery comes in at the door some of our wits fly out at the window.

   Aunt Abigail in *Understood Betsy,* by Dorothy Canfield Fisher

2. I declare! Sometimes it seems to me that every time a new piece of machinery comes in at the door some of our wits fly out at the window.

   Aunt Abigail in *Understood Betsy,* by Dorothy Canfield Fisher

3. I declare! Sometimes it seems to me that every time a new piece of machinery comes in at the door some of our wits fly out at the window.

   Aunt Abigail in *Understood Betsy,* by Dorothy Canfield Fisher

*The word "of" in #1 will bump down to the next line, as shown in #2, but we get an even better "rag" by narrowing the entire paragraph just a tiny bit so the lines break as shown in #3.*

. . . . . . . . . . . . . . . . . . . . . . . . . . . . . . . . . . . . . . . .

# Right aligned

Text aligned on the right creates a definite *look,* as shown below, quite different from left-aligned. The letter and word spacing still retain their ideal built-in settings, and corrections can often be made without affecting the rest of the text. The biggest drop in readability comes from the fact that the left edge, where your eye returns to find the next line to read, is not consistent so your eye has to find the beginning of the line again every time it moves to the left. In small amounts of text, this isn't a major problem, and the sacrifice can be worth it in exchange for the distinctive layout.

When you use a right alignment for the look it creates, then emphasize the look—don't be a wimp. Instead of keeping the ragged edge as smooth as possible, try exaggerating it.

There is no excuse for widows or hyphenated words when you set a right align-ment. Since you are determining the line endings and since this format is rarely used with an extended amount of text, you can help compensate for the lower readability by being thoughtful in the grouping of phrases. And while you're at it you can completely eliminate any hyphenation.

I'VE ALWAYS WANTED TO
BE SOMEBODY. BUT I CAN
SEE NOW I SHOULD HAVE
BEEN MORE SPECIFIC.
**Lily Tomlin**

I'VE ALWAYS WANTED
TO BE SOMEBODY.
BUT I CAN SEE NOW
I SHOULD HAVE BEEN
MORE SPECIFIC.
**Lily Tomlin**

*If you're going to align text on the right, don't try to disguise it. It's difficult to tell if the text above is supposed to be right-aligned or not. Typeface is Las Bonitas.*

*If you make the right alignment strong, it adds another dimension to the type and takes it beyond merely words on the page.*

# Center aligned

A centered alignment also gives a particular look to text: a more formal, sedate, and potentially more boring sort of look. People who are just beginning to work with text tend to center everything because it's safe. It's symmetrical. It fills the space, everything balances automatically. However, a centered alignment can create a dreadfully dull piece, and it often creates an amateurish page.

A centered alignment has consistent letter and word spacing, but you have to keep finding the beginning of the lines as you read so it is not the most readable arrangement. But if you're going to do it, then do it. Make it clear that the text is centered, not just poorly justified. Varying line lengths make the page visually interesting. Also, a centered alignment gives you a chance to group the lines into logical thoughts. And remember, there's never an excuse for hyphenated words.

*On with the dance! Let joy be unconfined;*
*No sleep til morn, when youth and pleasure meet*
*To chase the glowing hours with flying feet.*

*Lord Byron*

This is nice, but it doesn't have much strength or passion;
it's hard to tell the poem is centered.

*On with the dance!*
*Let joy be unconfined;*
*No sleep til morn, when youth and pleasure meet*
*To chase the glowing hours*
*with flying feet.*

*Lord Byron*

This layout has a much more intriguing shape.
Take advantage of the flexibility
of centered lines.
Also read "Consider those phrases" on page 124.
Typeface is General Menou.

· · · · · · · · · · · · · · · · · · · · · · · · · · · · · · · · · · · · · · · · · · · · · · · · · ·

# Justified

When you justify text, the computer forces the lines to extend to a certain length by adding or deleting space between the words, and sometimes between the letters. Some programs let you specify the minimum and maximum amounts the spacing can adjust, but the computer will override your specifications if necessary.

The greatest problem with justified text, both in terms of readability and aesthetics, is the uneven word spacing and letter spacing: some lines of text have extra spacing between the words and letters, some less. This irregularity is visually disturbing and interrupts reading. The shorter the line length in relation to the size of the type, the worse this problem becomes because there are fewer words between which to add or delete space (see below).

One simple rule for determining whether a line length is "long enough" to justify is this: The line length in picas should be at least twice the point size of the type: if you're using 12-point type, the minimum line length before you should try to justify is 24 picas (6 picas equal 1 inch). This line length you are reading is 28p6 (28 picas, 6 points), and the type size is 11/14.

For many years, justified type reigned supreme as the way to set most text. But the trend over the past couple of decades has been to allow the natural spacing of flush left text to dominate, losing the structured look of the "block" of text, but maximizing readability.

So sweet a kiss the golden sun gives not to those fresh morning drops upon the rose, as thy eye-beams, when their fresh rays have smote the night of dew that on my cheeks down flows: nor shines the silver moon one half so bright through the transparent bosom of the deep, as doth thy face through tears of mine give light; thou shinest in every tear that I do weep.

*Love's Labor's Lost*

So sweet a kiss the golden sun gives not to those fresh morning drops upon the rose, as thy eye-beams, when their fresh rays have smote the night of dew that on my cheeks down flows: nor shines the silver moon one half so bright through the transparent bosom of the deep, as doth thy face through tears of mine give light; thou shinest in every tear that I do weep.

*Love's Labor's Lost*

*Even with a long-enough line length, you will still get uneven word spacing when you justify the text. But notice how terrible the word spacing is in the example to the left—hold the page at an angle, squint, and you can see all the holes, and even "rivers" of white space running through the type. At least with a longer line, the gaps aren't so obvious. Typeface is Bembo.*

Logic only gives man what he needs.
Magic gives him what he wants.

Baba the Idiot

# Headlines and Subheads

The headlines and subheads in a document do more than simply give clues as to the content of the stories. They provide an organization to the page; they provide a repetitive element that unifies the publication; they provide the visual contrast that attracts our eyes to the page. Here are a few guidelines for using heads and subheads to effectively take advantage of their presence.

- **Avoid using all caps or small caps.** They are difficult to read, which defeats their purposes as headlines or subheads. Plus all caps take up too much space. Using lowercase letters, you will have more room to use a larger and bolder font.

- **Watch the leading** on multiple-line heads. The larger the type size, the less leading you need. If there are few or no descenders, it is particularly important to remove the excess space. Your intent is to keep the two lines together as one visual unit.

- **If your text is flush left,** keep your heads and subheads flush left, *not centered.* This is particularly important if your page feels a little cluttered; keeping the heads flush left with the text will reduce some of the visual clutter. When a head is centered, our eyes connect its placement with the first line of the first paragraph. If the first line of text does not stretch all the way across the column, the centered headline won't have a good connection to the story.

- **Don't indent the first paragraph in the story.** This is to preserve the strength of the alignment and to be typographically correct. Any indent you do use should be only about two spaces wide, about one em space (as wide as the point size of your type; see page 117).

- **There should always be a little more space** *above* a subhead than below it to ensure that the subhead is visually connected with the text it refers to. If the subhead is too far away, or if it is the same distance between the text above and below it, the subhead appears to be an unconnected, separate element.

- **Create a clear distinction between heads and subheads.** If the only difference between your head and subhead is size, then make sure they are significantly different sizes. You might want to italicize the subheads, or if you have a rule (a drawn line) beneath the headline, remove the line from the subhead.

- **Avoid awkward line breaks.** Read your heads and subheads carefully. Check for line breaks that might cause confusion or ambiguity. Make sure there are no silly line endings. And of course don't hyphenate.

- **Choose a typeface** for your heads and subheads that provides a strong contrast to your body text. This creates a contrast on the page that not only is visually attractive, but also strengthens the organization and makes a clearer path for the reader to follow.

Generally, your body text is a serif face, since extended amounts of text are easier to read with serifs. If so, a strong, bold sans serif is a good choice for heads and subheads. If you don't have a strong, bold face in your font library, you'll find that an investment in one is your single best investment toward more effective design and communication.

If your body text is a lightweight sans serif, the strong bold in the same font would work well for headlines. Just make sure there is a solid difference between the light weight and the heavy weight. For instance, the Helvetica Bold or Arial Bold that comes on your computer is not bold enough to stand out effectively.

You might also want to consider a heavy slab serif face as a headline type, which is so different in structure and weight from any readable sans serif or serif that it works well as a headline type with almost any face.

• • • • • • • • • • • • • • • • • • • • • • • • • • • • • • • • • • • • • • • • • • • • • • •

Now that you've read through the guidelines, circle the appropriate places in the story below where you see the principles being used. Not every single guideline has been used in this one example, of course. How many do you follow in your work?

## Giacche Enne Binnestaucche

Uans appona taim uasse disse boi. Neimmese Giacche. Naise boi. Live uite ise mamma. Mainde di cao.

Uane dei, di spaghetti ise olle aute. Dei gonna feinte fromme no fudde. Mamma sci sai, "Orai, Giacche, teicche di cao enne treide erre forre bocchese spaghetti enne somme uaine."

### Giacche commes

Bai enne bai commese Giacche. I garra no fudde, i garra no uaine. Meicchese mesteicche enne treidese di cao forre bonce binnese. Uate giacchesse!

Mamma, scise engri. Giompe appe enne daonne craine, "Uara iu, somme caine creisi?" Denne sci tro olle binnese aute di uindo. Necchese dei, Giacche lucchese aute enne uara iu tincche? Ise si disse binnestaucche uate ricce appe tru di claodese. Somme uide!

Giacche gose appe di binnestaucche. Ise disse ogghere! Ise menne nainti sicchese fit taulle uite tri grin aise! Enne i garra ghusse uate leise ghode egghese!

Giacche ielle "Ciao!" Denne ise grabbe di ghusse enne cuicche claime daonne fromme di binnestaucche. Ise go cioppe cioppe uite di acchese. Di nainti sicchese futte menne ise faulle enne breicche di necche. Auce!

### Cucchede ghusse

Mamma sci giompesse fromme gioi. Meicchese naise ghusse cacciatore. Bai enne bai, dei garra no morre fudde. Dei gonna dai! Uatsa iuse? Uara iu gonna du uenne iorre ghusse ise cucchede?

Many thanks to Michael Howley for passing this delightful story along to me!

*Typefaces are Eurostile in the heads and subheads, Bembo in the body copy.*

# Have fun with it!

If appropriate for your content, experiment with different ways of setting heads. Perhaps add a rule above and/or below the heads, or reverse them, set them extra large, or use an initial cap. If you have a special story, perhaps create a special headline. Keep in mind, though, that if every story has a special and different headline treatment, not one of them stands out as different or more important. Most stories should have typographically consistent headlines to retain the unity of the publication.

Always, always remember, your purpose is to communicate. No matter which technique you use, your heads and subheads should support that purpose.

*Headline typeface is Mister Frisky.*

# Pull Quotes

Many times you must design or write a page that has no accompanying graphic to lighten the page and make it more enticing to read. That's where **pull quotes** come in so handy. A pull quote is when you take a quote from an article, story, or dull report and emphasize it on the page in some graphic way (as shown below). There are many ways to do this, and this chapter shows you several examples and provides some basic guidelines.

Pull quotes are often seen in the middle of the page, but there is no rule to force you to do this. Try some variations, such as a flush right or left quote in a wide outer margin (flush with the column of text); a quote in a background that cuts into one column of text; or a quote that runs

**Evanescent wan think, itching udder.**

horizontally across 1.5 or 2 columns. Use interesting punctuation marks, such as ampersands or questions marks, as graphic elements; perhaps set them large or colorful.

On the following two pages are samples of pull quotes. Have fun with them, make them attractive—that's their point! Be sure to read page 134 for guidelines on working with pull quotes.

· · · · · · · · · · · · · · · · · · · · · · · · · · · · · · · · · · · · · · · · · · · · · · · · · · · · · ·

# Be creative!

More often than not, the purpose of a pull quote is to add some visual interest to the page. So do it. Make that pull quote beautiful, provocative, interesting, dynamic! This is not the place to be a wimp.

**"Wail, wail, wail," set disk wicket woof. "Evanescent Ladle Rat Rotten Hut."**

*A simple rule above and below the quote sets it apart. Notice the punctuation is hung off the left edge so the text retains its strong left alignment.*

*Typeface is Antique Olive Bold.*

**You can't let the seeds stop you from enjoyin' the watermelon.**

*With a colored or black box, you can inset this quote so it tucks halfway into the adjacent column and hangs halfway out into the margin.*

*Typeface is Antique Olive Compact.*

The harder you work, the luckier you get.

*Tall, narrow settings with lots of linespace work well in outer margins. Align the flush edge with the edge of the column. That is, the quote in the outer margin of the left-hand page should be flush right, aligned against the column of text. On the outer margin of a right-hand page, the quote should be flush left.*

*Typeface is Bernhard Modern.*

• • • • • • • • • • • • • • • • • • • • • • • • • • • • • • • • • • • • • •

Ιν Δεχεμβερ α γυψ δελιϖερεδ α βυνχη οφ ωοοδ τηατ ηε χηοππεδ ιν μψ δριϖεωαψ. Ηε χηοππεδ τηε πιεχεσ τοο βιγ το τ ιν μψ στοϖε. Ηε σα ιδ ηε ωουλδ ρε τυρν ανδ χ ηο π τηεμ σμρ αλ λερ. Ηε νϖερ διδ. Ι παιδ ηιμ ρεπ εϖεν τηουγη ηε ασκεδ φορ Συ βεχαυσε ιτ ωασ α λοτ οφ ωοοδ ανδ Ι διδντ ρεαλιζε ηοω μανψ πιεχεσ ωερε υνυσαβλε φορ με. Σο ηε σαιδ ηε ωουλδ βρινγ

με α λοαδ οφ κινδλινγ. Ηε βρουγητ οϖερ ειγητ ρεδειγητ ρεδωοοδ ρουνδσ, εαχη αβουτ φερ 18 ινχηεσ λονγ ανδ φδτηρεε φεετ αχροσσ. Ι κεπτ ωαιτινγ φορ τηε κινδλινγ ανδ ωηεν θιμμψ ναλλψ τολδ ηιμ Ι ωασ ωονδερινγ ωηερε τηε κινδλινγ ωασ, ηε σα ιδ τηε ρεδωοοδ ωασ τηε κινδλινγ. Ιϖε βεεν ωονδερινγ ηοω το γετ ριδ οφ ιτ.

> She claims the secret to success is understanding that
> **your attitude is your life.**

*Try a horizontal quote extending across several columns. As with all pull quotes, leave plenty of white space surrounding it. Typefaces are Antique Olive Light, Antique Olive Compact, and Symbol for the Greek text.*

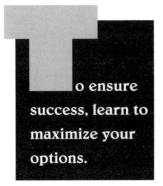

To ensure success, learn to maximize your options.

*Apply a gray shade or a pale color to large drop caps. This adds visual interest without overpowering the short quote.*

*Typeface is Belwe Medium for the body copy and Antique Olive Nord for the cap T.*

*full of* **sound & fury** *signifying nothing*

*Whenever possible and appropriate, take advantage of provocative punctuation and symbols.*

*Typeface is Antique Olive Nord with a Goudy Oldstyle Italic ampersand and text.*

· · · · · · · · · · · · · · · · · · · · · · · · · · · · · · · · · · · · · · · · · · · · · · · · · · · · · · · · ·

# Guidelines for pull quotes

Here are a few guidelines for setting pull quotes in your documents:

- Always hang the punctuation (see Chapter 5).
- Reduce the size of punctuation in large type.
- Use only one alignment; for instance, don't set part of the text flush right and part of it centered.
- Make centered type obviously centered; break the lines at logical endings to create an interesting visual arrangement.
- Position initial caps on one of the baselines.
- Create a style for your pull quotes and use it consistently throughout your publication.

# Captions

Captions are an important little feature of printed material. Every photo or illustrative figure should have an explanatory sentence or two accompanying it. People expect captions, so a photo without one confuses the reader momentarily. Often this explanatory text is the only thing people read. Take advantage of this fact, and don't let your captions be dull or useless—make them an integral part of the story and of the page design.

## Choosing a typeface

The typeface for captions should either be a member of the same font family as your body text, or a font that is very different. Don't choose a font that is different but similar to the body text!

For instance, if you are using Garamond for your body text, feel free to use Garamond Italic or Semibold for your captions. Keep in mind that many OpenType Pro fonts, especially the oldstyle serif faces, include a specially designed caption font, as explained in Chapter 8.

If you want to use another face altogether, choose something that is obviously different from your serif face, such as a sans serif—don't choose another serif. If you are using a sans serif typeface for your headlines, use a light weight of the same sans serif for the captions.

In my book, *The Non-Designer's Design Book,* the entire second half deals specifically with the problem of using more than one typeface on a page.

. . . . . . . . . . . . . . . . . . . . . . . . . . . . . . . . . . . . . . . . . . . . . . . . . . . .

# Choosing a type size and leading value

Captions are traditionally a bit smaller than the point size of the body copy, but keep in mind that many people read only the captions, so you don't want them to be difficult to read! Generally, use a size that is one to two points below the size of the body text (unless your body text is already tiny). If your body copy is 10 or 11 point, you can easily use 9- or 9.5-point caption type.

Alternatively, use the same size as your body text, but use the italic or semibold version of the font. You want it to be clear to the reader that these few lines are not meant to be in the flow of the story.

Your choice of leading value (linespace) depends on whether or not you are trying to align all your elements to a **grid:** Are you consciously aligning your baselines across columns? If so, your headlines must be set in a leading value, or linespace, that is a multiple of your body copy linespace.

> For instance, say your body copy is 10-point type with 12-point leading. If your heads have a *leading value* of 24 or 36 (two or three times the 12-point leading), all your text will always line up across columns. Your captions should follow the same guidelines— maintain that 12-point leading value.

> This assumes, of course, that you are indenting paragraphs instead of adding paragraph space between them.

If you are not forcing all elements into a grid format, then you have more flexibility with the leading value. Smaller type can usually get away with less leading. For instance, most faces at 9-point can get away with adding only a half a point or one point of linespace. Remember that sans serif faces need a little more linespace because their x-heights are usually larger than serif faces.

# Alignment

Whether or not you are using a grid, the baseline of your caption should be on the same baseline as the text in the nearest column. The bottom of your photograph or illustration should also be aligned with a baseline in the next column. *This arrangement must be consistent throughout your publication!*

An even more important alignment is the relationship between the text and the photo or illustration. If your body copy is flush left or justified, then your captions should be flush left with the edge of the photo! Don't center captions unless everything else on the page is centered! You see, most photos have a strong, hard edge along both sides, yes? Your body text also has a strong hard edge along its side, yes? So don't weaken those clean lines by centering your captions—follow and increase the strength of those edges by aligning the caption with them.

Ms. Isabella Melanzana
will be speaking
at our next meeting.

▶ A strange figure was discovered
in the office late last night.

*See the nice straight edge along the left side of this column? Follow that alignment with your caption! Don't weaken the entire page by centering your captions and losing the strength of that alignment.*

*Typeface is Memphis Light.*

*If you have some sort of detail you are using as a repetitive element throughout your publication, perhaps use it also in your captions. For instance, in the document from which the above graphic was taken, there are lists that use triangles as bullets. The triangle has been pulled into the caption as a unifying element.*

*Typeface is Formata.*

. . . . . . . . . . . . . . . . . . . . . . . . . . . . . . . . . . . . . . . . . . . . . . . . . . . . .

# Be consistent

Whatever you're doing with your captions, be consistent. Don't confuse your reader; be thoughtful. Use the same alignment, typeface and style, size and leading. Be consistent about the placement—such as how far below the bottom edge of the photograph you place it, or aligning it with a baseline. Use a style sheet for the captions. (If you don't know how to use the style sheets in your application, you must learn! Style sheets are one of the most important features you can master.)

There are little tricks in every application for ensuring that the placement of captions is consistent—ask other people who use the same page layout application what tricks they use.

# Emphasizing Type

Every page of type contains at least a few words or headlines that need to stand out, either because they are important to the content, or perhaps the words need to be emphasized to add enough visual interest to the page so a reader is attracted to it. No matter what the reason, there are appropriate and inappropriate ways to call attention to particular words.

## DON'T DO THIS

The inappropriate ways of emphasizing certain words or phrases are generally holdovers from using the typewriter, when our only options were to type words in ALL CAPS or <u>underline them.</u> Rarely should you use all caps, and never should you underline words in print. Never. That's a law.

When words are set in all caps, we lose the recognition of the shape of the word and are forced to read the word letter by letter (how many times have you read that now?). For instance, the word "cat" in lowercase has a different shape from the word "dog," and that shape helps us identify it. When the words CAT or DOG are set in all caps, their rectangular shapes are identical.

## Italic, not underline

Typewriters, obviously, could not type in italic, so an underline on a typewriter was meant to fake an italic; that's why you were taught to type book titles with underlines, and why you underlined words in mid-paragraph when you wanted to emphasize them. But on your computer you have true typesetting choices—you don't have to fake it anymore, you can actually type in italic. Besides, the underline is usually too close to the bottoms of the letters and actually cuts into the descenders. And <u>*underlining*</u> an italic word is simply redundant.

· · · · · · · · · · · · · · · · · · · · · · · · · · · · · · · · · · · · · · · · · · · · · · · · ·

# But you *can* do this

You have other options for emphasizing type that will create a more sophisticated or exciting typographic look, as well as help in the organization of information.

Using *italic* instead of an underline, where appropriate, is one way you can emphasize text in a subtle way, of course. For a stronger emphasis, use the boldest version of the typeface, or perhaps the ***bold italic.***

For a more dramatic emphasis, use a different typeface altogether, one that has a strong contrast to the rest of the text. For instance, if your text is a classic oldstyle face (like what you're reading right now), use a very bold sans serif for **emphasis.**

But don't use a weight that is *similar* to the other text, especially for headlines—notice how much more effective the emphasis is when the sans serif is a strong black, as above.

If you have the opportunity to use another color, take advantage of that color in your text or headlines when you need an emphasis. Just remember that the less that second color appears, the more dramatic the emphasis will be. Warm colors (reds, oranges) are the strongest, and very little goes a long way (and it's very easy to have too much). Cool colors (blues, greens) recede, and you can use more of them without overwhelming the page.

. . . . . . . . . . . . . . . . . . . . . . . . . . . . . . . . . . . . . . . . . . . . . . . . .

# Add space

If your design allows, add empty space around the text to immediately draw more attention to it. I know, your boss doesn't like empty space—she says that she paid for it and she wants to use it. But think of those ads in magazines or newspapers where there is nothing at all except a few words in the middle of the page. Ask your boss if she noticed that ad. Ask her if she read that ad. Ask her if it is possible for anyone to open to that page and *not* read that ad.

No it is not.

The boss who had the courage to pay for all that space and let it be empty had the highest readership of any page in that entire publication. When there is clutter, our eyes are attracted to the resting places of the blankness. Have courage. Let the white space be there. Do you notice how much attention is called to that one line above, "No it is not"? It appears very important because of all the empty, white space surrounding it. In fact, you probably read *that* line before you read the paragraphs on this page.

## Rules and size can be effective

You don't ever want to use the underline feature in your software, but you can often apply a rule, or line, for emphasis, as shown in the headline above (in most programs you can add the rule to your style sheet so it shows up automatically). The advantage to the rule is that you can make it as thick or thin as you like, and you can make it a different color, dotted, or dashed. You can position the rule so it doesn't bump into the descenders, or, as you see in the running heads on each page, you can let it run through the descenders in exactly the position you choose.

**Or:**

Of course you know you can emphasize type by making it bigger. But don't be a wimp—try making it *really* big, making the letterforms themselves into a design element, or perhaps enlarging just the interesting punctuation such as the question mark or ampersand or quotation marks. Or try setting the text very small, surrounded by lots of space. Either choice, large or small, will call a great deal of attention to itself.

So stretch yourself—go beyond the basic italic or bold word.

# Be emphatic!

# Line Breaks and Hyphenation

Your design project is complete. Graphics are in place, colors have been chosen, paper has been selected, your client has signed off on the project, it's ready to go to press. But you need to check one last thing—your line breaks, or how each line of type ends. Yes, that means every line in your entire project, every headline, every caption, every line in every paragraph! Certain elements are inappropriate at the ends of lines, such as too many hyphens, small words that hang over an empty space in the next line, awkward phrases, the last half of a hyphenated word as the last line of a paragraph, among others. These are details that might not seem important at first, but these details are what give your document or your publication a professional, polished, and precise appearance.

*See, isn't that line break tacky?!*

Yes, checking every line break can be time-consuming, but it will give your publications that added touch of professionalism.

· · · · · · · · · · · · · · · · · · · · · · · · · · · · · · · · · · · · · · · · · · · · · · · · · · · · · ·

# How to fix line breaks

Sometimes the easiest and best way to fix bad line breaks, especially if they involve long words that are hard to manage, is to have editing privileges: change a long word to a short word, or a short word to a long one; rephrase the sentence; eliminate superfluous words. But since that is not always possible, here are a few other tricks for adjusting the ends of your lines:

- Most software packages that work with text have a *line break* feature, sometimes called a "soft return." Instead of hitting the Return or Enter key, you hit Shift Return/Enter or perhaps Option Return or Alt Enter. This creates a hard line break, but it does not pick up any of the paragraph formatting you would get with a Return, such as extra space before or after, or a first-line indent or a style change.

- Most packages also have a *discretionary hyphen,* affectionately called a "dischy." You've probably noticed hyphens that occasionally appear in the middle of words in the middle of sentences (where someone manually hyphen-ated the word at the end of a sentence, later edited the sentence, and the hyphen stuck). Well, if you use a discretionary hyphen, usually by typing Command or Control Hyphen instead of the plain ol' hyphen, that hyphen will disappear when the word moves to another location. Check the manual for your software.

  Also (and this is the point), if you *type a discretionary hyphen in front of a hyphenated word,* it will not hyphenate at all, ever. Use this to make sure you never end up with a hyphen in the middle of the text, as shown above. Also use it so names of people or places don't hyphenate.

- You can often use subtle kerning or tracking in a line or in a few words, just enough to bring up the end of a hyphenated word.

- Try widening or narrowing the column just a tiny bit. Especially if it is set rag right, the difference won't be noticeable.

- For one-liners that are a bit too long, such as headlines or index entries or parts lists, try justifying the line. This will often squeeze ornery text onto one line.

# What are bad line breaks?

Look for bad line breaks throughout every line of body copy. Of course, *do this only on final copy,* after all editing has been done! Here are several examples of the sorts of things to look for:

**Casing Adder Bat** ❶

Heresy borsch-boil starry a ❷ boarder borsch boil gam plate lung, lung a gore in- ❸ ner ladle wan-hearse torn coiled Mutt-fill.

Mutt-fill worsen mush of- ❹ fer torn, butted hatter putty gut borsch-boil tame, an off oiler pliers honor tame, door moist cerebrated worse Cas- ❺ ing. Casing worsted sickened basement, any hatter betting orphanage off .526 (fife toe sex). ❻

Casing worse gut lurking an furry poplar—spatially wetter gull coiled Any-bally. Any-bally worse Casing's sweat-hard, any harpy cobble wandered toe gat merit, ❼ bought Casing worse toe pore toe becalm Any-bally's ❽ horsebarn. (Boil pliers honor Mutt-fill tame dint gat mush offer celery; infect, day gut nosing atoll.)

Butt less gat earn wetter star- ❾ ry.

**Casing Adder Bat**

Heresy borsch-boil starry a boarder borsch boil gam plate lung, lung a gore inner ladle wan-hearse torn coiled Mutt-fill.

Mutt-fill worsen mush offer torn, butted hatter putty gut borsch-boil tame, an off oiler pliers honor tame, door moist cerebrated worse Casing. Casing worsted sickened basement, any hatter betting orphanage off .526 (fife toe sex).

Casing worse gut lurking an furry poplar—spatially wetter gull coiled Any-bally. Any-bally worse Casing's sweat-hard, any harpy cobble wandered toe gat merit, bought Casing worse toe pore toe becalm Any-bally's horsebarn. (Boil pliers honor Mutt-fill tame dint gat mush offer celery; infect, day gut nosing atoll.)

Bought less gat earn wetter darn starry.

❶*Justify the headline so it stays on one line.* ❷*Use a line break (Shift Return/Enter) to bump "a" down to the next line, where it fits very nicely.* ❸*Kern the line a tiny bit to bring the rest of the word up.* ❹*Type a dischy in front of the word to bump it down.* ❺*Never hyphenate a person's name. I had to go up a few lines, bump "off" down, which bumped the other line endings down. This also took care of the inappropriate widow in* ❻*.* ❼*There is plenty of room to squeeze "bought" on this line, perhaps by kerning the line a tiny bit.* ❽*"Horsebarn" is a good long word that could be hyphenated; type a dischy. Better yet, when "bought" moved up, it gave enough room to move "horsebarn" up. If that doesn't work, try opening the text block or text box a wee bit.* ❾*Edit: to get rid of that terrible widow, exchange a short word for a long word.*     Story is by Howard L. Chace.

· · · · · · · · · · · · · · · · · · · · · · · · · · · · · · · · · · · · · · · · ·

# Headlines

Don't hyphenate headlines. That's a law.

**Don Quixote de la Man-cha**

*Don't laugh—I have actually seen this as a printed headline.*

Also, watch where the first line of a two-line headline ends—does it create a silly or misleading phrase? Fix it.

**Professor and The-rapist to Lecture**

**Don't Lose Your Self Respect**

Don't leave widows (very short last lines) in headlines, especially when they leave a misleading phrase behind.

**Man Walks Barefoot Across Bay Bridge**

Fix it either way, or rewrite!

**Man Walks Barefoot across Bay Bridge**

**Man Walks Barefoot across Bay Bridge**

. . . . . . . . . . . . . . . . . . . . . . . . . . . . . . . . . . . . . . . . . . . . .

# Captions

Generally captions don't need to stretch all the way across a column width. This flexibility gives you the freedom to break lines at appropriate places to create sensible phrasing. This is especially true if you center captions—you don't want all the lines the same length anyway.

Breaking sentences into complete phrases creates a more readable caption, and since many people read only the captions, it behooves you to make them as readable as possible.

Will Rogers said, "We can't all be heroes because someone has to sit on the curb and clap as they go by."

*Why hyphenate in a caption?*

Will Rogers said, "We can't all be heroes because
someone has to sit on the curb and clap as they go
by."

*There is no excuse to leave a widow in a caption!*

Will Rogers said, "We can't all be heroes because someone
has to sit on the curb and clap as they go by."

Will Rogers said, "We can't all be heroes because
someone has to sit on the curb and clap as they go by."

*These last two would not look good as paragraphs, but
would work fine aligned under a photograph or illustration.*

. . . . . . . . . . . . . . . . . . . . . . . . . . . . . . . . . . . . . . . . . . . . . . . . . .

# Hyphenation

If your text is flush left, right, or centered, hyphenation isn't a big problem. The only rule is to watch out for too many hyphens in a row and word breaks that are too short. Personally, my preference is never to allow more than one hyphenation in a row, and preferably no more than one in a paragraph. Other people whose opinions I respect are comfortable with, say, no more than three in a row. Also personally, I abhor those hyphenations that leave one or two letters at either end of the line. Others don't mind. No one, however, finds a hyphenated word as the last word in a paragraph to be acceptable.

If you are going to *justify* your text, you have other considerations to weigh because the computer hyphenates words in an attempt to maintain the most even word spacing possible. It's impossible to have totally even word spacing in justified text—the computer has to unnaturally force words to the beginnings and ends of the lines.

There are two schools of thought on justification with hyphenation: Some people are willing to put up with lots of hyphenated words, including two-letter ones, to ensure that the word spacing is as even as possible. Others are willing to accept uneven word spacing in exchange for fewer obnoxious hyphens at the ends of the lines—hyphens that interrupt the flow and color of the text much more than does a subtle change in or less-than-ideal word spacing. Guess to which school I belong? Guess which paragraph on this page makes me twitch with horror?

You can set your page layout application to get the effect you want. I have Adobe InDesign set to not allow hyphenations that would occur within three picas of the end of the line (depending on the length of my line), thereby eliminating two-letter breaks, and to not allow more than one hyphen in a row. You can usually add the hyphenation controls to your style sheets.

# Special Effects

In which we experiment
with ornaments
and dingbats,
swash characters,
initial caps, and
black-and-white "color"
in type, as well as
effective ways to use
distressed typefaces.

In mAtters
of grave importance,
"STyLE ";"
not sincerity,
is the
Vital thing.

Oscar Wilde
*The Importance of Being Earnest*

# Swash Characters

Have you ever wanted to give an extra-special look to some type without being too bold? Perhaps you want a strong yet elegant look? A judicious use of swash characters can add a touch of sophistication to headlines, titles, quotations, etc.

Swash characters are specially designed letterforms that have "tails" or elaborate shapes, usually swooping away from or under the rest of the letters. Swash characters are like cheesecake—use them sparingly for a delectable (not disgusting) effect. In the three examples below, the first one is the regular face, the second is the italic version, and the third is a combination of the italic and its matching swash font.

### Kissing Potion    *Kissing Potion*

### *Kissing ❤ Potion*

Swash characters are not included in most regular font character sets—you must buy a specially designed swash font in conjunction with your text font. Some OpenType families, especially the Pro versions, include swash characters in the italic font. The example above is a PostScript family called Zapf Renaissance Light and Light Italic, with a special swash face designed to complement them called Zapf Renaissance Light Italic Swash. You need to use the faces in combination with each other. It's common to use the italic swash with the regular face as well as with the italic face.

Many swash faces also contain a set of ornaments that can be used to complement the type. Their proportions and style are designed to work smoothly with the text. Several of them are used in this chapter, but also see Chapter 26 for details on ornaments and dingbats.

The Character Palette in Mac OS X and Character Map on the pc show the characters available in OpenType and swash fonts and allow you to insert them in applications that are programmed to accept them. See Chapter 8.

# Guidelines for using swashes

There are a few guidelines to follow when working with swash characters:

- Please, don't *ever* set text in all capital swash characters.

  *OH MY GRACIOUS THIS LOOKS SO STUPID!*

  Besides looking stupid, it is also dreadfully difficult to read.

- Swashes are designed to add elegant curves *to otherwise empty spaces,* such as under or over letters or at the beginnings or ends of sentences. So don't insert the kind of swash in the middle a word that creates an unsightly gap, or even at the end of a word in mid-sentence if it disturbs the word spacing.

  *He r spe cia lty was an alyzin g goblins.*

- In a typeface that imitates handwriting, swash characters can add to the effect of a personalized note, making it look handlettered. Below, the typeface General Menou includes many alternate and swash characters (notice the alternate characters for d, s, e, and g, among others). But don't limit a handlettered face such as this to only personal notes! General Menou is so beautiful it could easily be used for any elegant occasion.

  *Dear John,*

  *I miss you. Wish you could have dinner with me tonight at Rancho de Chimayó, with dessert in front of the fire and the snow falling outside.*

  *Love, R.*

• If you are going to use another typeface on the same page as the swash face, be careful. Avoid faces with similar characteristics, such as any other italic or script. Either stay in the same family, such as the Zapf Renaissance family, or choose a font that has strong contrasts (such as thicker strokes or a roman or sans serif or monoweight font).

• Don't overdo the number of swashes. As you've seen, swash characters add elegance only if they are used with discretion.

• The Character Palette in Mac OS X (see page 87) shows all the characters available in a font. On a PC, use the Character Map (see page 228). The Glyphs palette in InDesign offers easy access to all the alternate characters in a font; see Chapter 8.

• OpenType fonts can include a wide variety of swash characters and contextual and stylistic alternate characters. InDesign can automatically insert these characters for you, but you'll prefer to use more discretion.

*What a Time to Be Me!*

*What a Time to Be Me!*

*What a Time to Be Me!*

*What a Time to Be Me!*

*Above is Ministry Script, a gorgeous OpenType font from Veer.com.*

*In the first example, I turned off InDesign's "Discretionary Ligatures" and "Swash" options for OpenType.*

*In the second example, I turned on the OpenType option of automatic insertion of "Discretionary Ligatures" and "Swashes."*

*The third example has automatic insertion of "Discretionary Ligatures" and "Contextual Alternates," but not "Swashes."*

*In the last example I used InDesign's Glyphs palette and was selective about which alternate characters to use.*

## Don't be a wimp

Don't be shy! If you find a swash or two that is exceptionally beautiful, set it extraordinarily large and use it as a graphic element on your page—show it off! Set it in a pale color or a shade of grey and let it swoop under your body text or behind a photograph. Use a huge swash character as an initial cap or as a lead-in to an article or chapter. Combine one large italic swash character with heavy, bold, black sans serif characters for a striking contrast in a title or quote. Look through this book and take note of where and how I've used swash characters. Oh, the possibilities are endless and exciting!

*Lord, what fools these Mortals be!*

*Puck in A Midsummer Night's Dream*

*Typeface is General Menou.*

# Initial Caps

LARGE OR ORNATE LETTERS at the beginning of first paragraphs, also called initial caps or drop caps, not only add interest to a page, but help guide the reader's eyes and pull the reader into the text. There are many ways to create an initial cap, as shown in the examples following. Be brave, be strong, be big where appropriate. Here are just a couple of simple guidelines to remember.

- The baseline of most initial caps or the bottom of the graphic image belonging to the initial cap should align with one of the baselines of the text.

- Don't overdo it. One initial cap is beautiful; an initial cap beginning every paragraph on the page is redundant and destroys the effect. Sometimes on a text-heavy page you can use two or three initial caps in lieu of graphics or pullquotes, but be aware of their impact and don't overdose the reader.

For only the very young
saw Life ahead, and only
the very old saw Life behind;
the others between were
so busy with Life
they saw nothing.

Ray Bradbury

Typeface is Isadora.

· · · · · · · · · · · · · · · · · · · · · · · · · · · · · · · · · · · · · · · · · · · · · · · · ·

# Examples of initial caps

There is a wonderful variety of ways to use initial caps. Here are several examples, which I hope will inspire you to play and create even greater and more interesting ways to use them.

**S**ometimes the seas are calm,
and that's wonderful.
Sometimes the seas are not calm,
and that's the way it is.
Rabbi Nathan Seagull

*Typeface is Bodoni Poster Compressed.*

*In InDesign, I set the letter "O" in a text block of its own so I could custom text wrap it. Typeface is Schmelvetica.*

**O** time, strength, cash, and patience! Small erections may be finished by their first architects; grand ones, true ones, ever leave the copestone to posterity. God keep me from ever completing anything.    Herman Melville, *Moby Dick*

*I set the "W" separately from the text. I used the Direct Selection Tool (the white pointer) in InDesign to reshape the text block with an angle on the left to match the angle of the W. Typefaces are Belwe Condensed and Light.*

**W**hen I'm in a good space, I see obstructions as instructions. When I am in a bad space, even instructions look like obstructions.
Norm Howe

*Typefaces are Printers Ornaments M for the decorative block, Dear Sarah for the cap "I" and byline, and DeconStruct Medium for the body copy.*

**I**n the midst of all the doubts which we have discussed for four thousand years in four thousand ways, the safest course is still to do nothing against one's conscience.
*Voltaire*

• • • • • • • • • • • • • • • • • • • • • • • • • • • • • • • • • • • • • • • • •

Letters sometimes give ear to a disturbing tremor which seismically runs the gamut of the entire alphabet. They are plagued by the lascivious laughter of the old satyrs of the woods and the painful cries of the dying. In the valleys of rich abundance and in their dwelling house, the atmosphere seems to them suffocatingly oppressive.

One unforgettable night they quit with light abandon the heavy encumbrance of words to seek the wordless heights where the air is purer and the horizon infinite. They have been freed by the whim of a capricious god. The great silence of the heights feels like a soothing caress across the feverish brow . . .

they have reached the top of the mountain and fulfilled the longing of a lifetime.

But, should they remain there until the dawn streaks the sky, they will be torn to pieces by the wolf of abstractions. In a frightened, concerted mass, they rush down the slopes, bleating miserably. Only when they reach the sanctuary of the pen do they feel happy and secure.

One of them, however, stands with its nose pressed between the bars of the closed gate; it is the O, longing to return to the mountain heights.

*Olof Lagercrantz*

*If the text is rather playful, experiment with lots of initial caps. Experiment with pale colors or tints, and don't let them overwhelm the body copy. Try letting the pale initial caps slide under the text above them, as on page 155. Typefaces are Eurostile Bold Condensed and Caslon Pro Regular.*

*Notice I kerned the cap "T" out to the left a little so its stem aligned with the cap "I" in the next line. Typeface is Bernhard Bold Condensed.*

**Take it as it comes. If it doesn't come, go get it. If you can't get it, create it.**

The ditches were rushing rivers; the ponds were full, the earth was already turning green, the swish of the rain upon the trees was terrific; but deafening, drowning all other noises was the ecstatic chorus of millions of frogs from every ditch and pond and field and compound, a wild, mad, maddening, corybantic, croaking and creaking orgasm of sound of wet, wallowing frogs.

Leonard Woolf

*Typefaces are Fantasia Initial Caps for the cap "T" (which is actually an EPS file) and Dirty One for the body copy.*

· · · · · · · · · · · · · · · · · · · · · · · · · · · · · · · · · · · · · · · · · · · · · · · · · ·

# Automatic drop caps

 AGE layout applications can apply drop caps (one form of initial caps) automatically. You can determine how many characters drop down and how many lines they drop. The drop cap in this paragraph is from Massele, a set of EPS initial caps from Aridi.com. They have a wonderful variety of sets. I inserted the graphic as the first character of the paragraph, and InDesign just accepts it and applies the drop cap specs to it.

> **InDesign:** Use the two "Drop Cap" fields in the Paragraph palette. Set the number of lines the cap is to drop into the text, and the number of characters you want to act as drop caps.
>
> **PageMaker:** Use the "Drop Cap" plug-in from the Utilities menu.
>
> **QuarkXPress:** Look in the Formats dialog box under the Style menu.

Also take a look at the initial letters offered by many font vendors. Many come as graphics in EPS format (as the one shown in the first paragraph, above, and on the previous page), which means you can text wrap them, color them, or resize them endlessly. There are some incredibly beautiful caps to choose from—get a set and see what they inspire.

# Everything must end. Meanwhile, we must amuse ourselves.

**Voltaire**

*This is a drop cap created instantly in InDesign using the Drop Cap feature. Typeface is Jim Casual.*

# Typographic Color

Typographers have always referred to black-and-white type on a page as having "color." It's easy to create contrast with paintbox colors; it takes a more sophisticated eye to see and take advantage of the color contrasts in black-and-white. Often, black and white are the only "colors" available, but don't let that limit you—this chapter will give you some ideas to use to ferment your own.

A gray, text-only page can be very dull to look at and uninviting to read. I'm sure you've opened up newsletters or technical documents and found these dull pages, or perhaps you've had to create them. It's not always possible to have graphics on a page to break up the text, but something needs to be done. A gray page can also create confusion by not giving the reader any clue as to the importance of a story or whether two separate stories on the page are related to each other. An effective typographic technique to aid in the organization of a page is to add "color."

Just as the voice adds emphasis
to important words,
so can type:
**it shouts or whispers by variation of size.**

Just as the pitch of the voice
adds interest to the words,
so can type:
**it modulates by lightness or darkness.**

Just as the voice adds color
to the words by inflection,
so can type:
**it defines elegance, dignity, toughness
by choice of face.**

Jan White

*It's pretty easy to see what is creating the different colors in the typefaces above. Not only is it the weight of the stroke, but also the structure of the letterforms: tall and condensed vs. long and squatty. Also notice the color of the lightweight text in the example compared to the body copy in the paragraphs above. Typefaces are Eurostile Condensed and Eurostile Bold Extended Two.*

# What makes "color"?

The color of a typeface is determined by a combination of details: the space between the letters and between the lines, the space built into each character, the x-height, the thickness of the strokes, the serifs or lack of serifs, etc. A light, airy typeface with lots of letter spacing and linespacing creates a very light color (and texture). A bold sans serif, tightly packed, creates a dark color (with a different texture). You can clearly see the contrast of colors in the samples below.

In the time of your life, live . . . so that in that wondrous time you shall not add to the misery and sorrow of the world, but smile to the infinite delight and mystery of it.
William Saroyan

*Caslon Regular 8.5/10.5*

In the time of your life, live . . . so that in that wondrous time you shall not add to the misery and sorrow of the world, but smile to the infinite delight and mystery of it.
William Saroyan

*DeconStruct Bold 8.5/9.5*

In the time of your life, live . . . so that in that wondrous time you shall not add to the misery and sorrow of the world, but smile to the infinite delight and mystery of it.
William Saroyan

*Dear Sarah 10/10.5*

In the time of your life, live . . . so that in that wondrous time you shall not add to the misery and sorrow of the world, but smile to the infinite delight and mystery of it.
William Saroyan

*Memphis Medium 8.5/9*

In the time of your life, live . . . so that in that wondrous time you shall not add to the misery and sorrow of the world, but smile to the infinite delight and mystery of it.
William Saroyan

*Bernhard Regular 8.5/12*

In the time of your life, live . . . so that in that wondrous time you shall not add to the misery and sorrow of the world, but smile to the infinite delight and mystery of it.
William Saroyan

*Jimbo Condensed  8.5/10.5*

In the time of your life, live . . . so that in that wondrous time you shall not add to the misery and sorrow of the world, but smile to the infinite delight and mystery of it.
William Saroyan

*Regular Joe 8.5/10.5*

In the time of your life, live . . . so that in that wondrous time you shall not add to the misery and sorrow of the world, but smile to the infinite delight and mystery of it.
William Saroyan

*Times Roman 8.5/10.5*

In the time of your life, live . . . so that in that wondrous time you shall not add to the misery and sorrow of the world, but smile to the infinite delight and mystery of it.
William Saroyan

*Flyer ExtraBlack Condensed 8.5/10.5*

# Why use black-and-white color?

If you add color to your heads and subheads by using a typeface with a heavier weight, or if you perhaps set a quote or a passage or a short story in a different "color" (as in a pull quote), the page becomes more visually appealing. If it's visually appealing, readers are more likely to stop on a page and actually read it. And that's the point, right?

Besides making the page more inviting to read, this change in color also helps organize the information. Below, which of the two arrangements gives you an instant visual impression of what's going on, as opposed to having to read the actual text to see what the organization is?

**Center Alley**

Center Alley worse jester pore ladle gull hoe lift wetter stop-murder an toe heft-cisterns. Daze worming war furry wicket an shellfish parsons, spatially dole stop-murder, hoe dint lack Center Alley an, infect, word orphan traitor pore gull mar lichen ammonol dinner hormone bang.

Oily inner moaning disk wicket oiled worming shorted, "Center Alley, gad otter bet an goiter wark! Suture lacy ladle bomb! Shaker lake!" An firm moaning tell gnat disk ratchet gull word heifer wark lacquer hearse toe kipper horsing ardor, washer heft-cistern's closing, maker bets, gore tutor star fur perversions, cooker males, washer dashes, an doe oily udder hoard wark. Nor wander pore Center Alley worse tarred an disgorged!

**Hormone Derange**

O gummier hum warder buffer-lore rum Enter dar enter envelopes ply, Ware soiled'em assured adage cur-itching ward An disguise earn it clotty oil die. Harm, hormone derange, Warder dare enter envelopes ply, Ware soiled'em assured adage cur-itching ward An disguise earn it clotty oil die.

*With this page being so dull and gray, it is not instantly clear whether there are two separate stories, or perhaps they are both part of the same one. And the page has no contrast to attract your eyes.*

*Typefaces are Caslon Pro Regular and Bold.*

**Center Alley**

Center Alley worse jester pore ladle gull hoe lift wetter stop-murder an toe heft-cisterns. Daze worming war furry wicket an shellfish parsons, spatially dole stop-murder, hoe dint lack Center Alley an, infect, word orphan traitor pore gull mar lichen ammonol dinner hormone bang.

Oily inner moaning disk wicket oiled worming shorted, "Center Alley, gad otter bet an goiter wark! Suture lacy ladle bomb! Shaker lake!" An firm moaning tell gnat disk ratchet gull word heifer wark lacquer hearse toe kipper horsing ardor, washer heft-cistern's closing, maker bets, gore tutor star fur perversions, cooker males, washer dashes, an doe oily udder hoard wark. Nor wander pore Center Alley worse tarred an disgorged!

**Hormone Derange**

O gummier hum warder buffer-lore rum

Enter dar enter envelopes ply.

Ware soiled'em assured adage cur-itching ward

An disguise earn it clotty oil die.

Harm, hormone derange,

Warder dare enter envelopes ply.

Ware soiled'em assured adage cur-itching ward

An disguise earn it clotty oil die.

*The "color" now does two things: It attracts your eyes to the page, and makes it clear that there are two separate stories. Can you see what is creating the different "colors" of type?*

*Typefaces added are variations of Eurostile.*

*Stories are by Howard L Chace.*

Please keep in mind that there are certainly times when you want a lovely, elegant, subdued page with no strong contrast. Using many of the techniques in this book, you can also create that look. Whether you include contrast or not, creating an elegant page takes time and thought.

· · · · · · · · · · · · · · · · · · · · · · · · · · · · · · · · · · · · · · · · · · · · · · · · · · · · ·

# Color as in crayons

"Color" is a term with various interpretations, one of them, obviously, being color. When you are using actual colors, like those in a crayon box, an important thing to keep in mind is that warm colors (reds, oranges) come forward and command our attention. Our eyes are very attracted to warm colors, so it takes very little red to create a contrast, to catch your eye, to lead you around the page. It is easy to overdose on warm colors by applying too much in too many places. I know you paid for that second color, but I guarantee it will be more effective if you use it in small doses. I also know it is hard to convince your boss of that. Find examples of where color has been used sparingly to great effect and keep those examples in a file. Also find samples of color being used obnoxiously. I have a newsletter in my file that uses a second color of an ugly red—this ugly red covers more than half the newsletter, defeating the purpose of using color to make important items stand out.

Cool colors (blues, greens), on the other hand, recede from our eyes. You can get away with larger areas of a cool color; in fact, sometimes you *need* more of a cool color to create an effective contrast on the page. But even with cool colors, if the point of the color is to emphasize a point or to add a sophisticated splash, less is usually more.

*Scribble some red color in this little shape. Hold the page up and glance at it. Where does your eye land first? Tiny spots of color are powerful.*

# Ornaments & Dingbats

Ornaments and dingbats are delightful and easy ways to add visual interest to your pages. They are simply little decorative elements you can set along with your type because they are characters in the font. OpenType fonts and expert sets often have ornaments as extra characters. You can also buy entire sets of them as typefaces. What's the difference between ornaments and dingbats? It's a fuzzy line, but you might say that dingbats are the sorts of little elements you would use as bullets, whereas ornaments are more sophisticated decorations for more elegant type. But then again you might also say the two are the same. One use for ornaments or dingbats is as you see here—markers that indicate new paragraphs without actually making a paragraph space or indent. This can be an interesting effect for a short amount of copy, but more than one page of it would be difficult to plow through. Notice I added more linespace to this page, in addition to the ornaments; this was to lighten the color (see the previous chapter) and give a more inviting, open look to this solid block of text that really should be several short paragraphs.

---

Oh for a Muse of fire, that would ascend
the brightest heaven of invention.

Chorus in Henry V

# Other uses for ornaments and dingbats

Here are several other ideas for using ornaments. Once you own a font or two of dingbats and ornaments, you will discover all sorts of places to throw them in. Don't be a wimp.

- It is very common to see an ornament at the end of a magazine story indicating the end of that article. If you decide to use this technique, be consistent with the ornament so readers know what to expect when they see the mark. ❀

- Use ornaments in pull quotes to set the text apart, as on the previous page. This can be a beautiful and interesting alternative to a simple rule (line).

- Also experiment with using special dingbats as bullets in a list of items, or in a row as a border.

- Try throwing playful dingbats into your memos, letters, faxes, and other correspondence. There is no excuse for being dull. ☞

- Use a repetitive pattern of dingbats as a background texture, as shown below. Because the dingbats are a font, you can easily resize them, space them, and adjust their linespacing to make the pattern as light or dense as you like.

*Typeface is Pierre Bonnard.*

# Pi & Picture Fonts

Pi (pronounced "pie"), pictograph, and picture fonts are similar to ornaments and dingbats (see the previous chapter) except that they tend to be more specific. Many smaller vendors provide these specialty fonts that don't enjoy a large market, and they are often just what you need for a particular project. There is a font for just about everything. If you need a specialty font, order the catalogs of the smaller vendors (check Appendix B at the back of this book for vendor addresses).

## Pi fonts

A pi font is a special typeface with mathematical and scientific characters, indispensable for use in technical manuals or scientific treatises. What a blessing these fonts can be! And beyond the obvious practical use, many of these characters are interesting symbols that can be used in other ways. If you have one, print up all the characters and keep your eyes open for creative new ways to use them.

*What would you do if you needed these characters and didn't have this font!*
*Typefaces are Mathematical Pi 5 and Mathematical Pi 6.*

*These can come in handy when writing technical manuals.*
*There is also a companion font to this set that displays all the*
*other keys, such as Shift, Control, Command, and the rest.*
*Typefaces are PIXymbols Stylekey and PIXymbols Function.*

# Pictograph fonts

Similar to pi fonts are pictograph fonts, which provide international symbols. Many of these symbols are so interesting that they beg to be used in ways you might not immediately think of: in logos, perhaps, or as identifying organizational symbols in a brochure or annual report, or as decorative elements on their own.

*If you ever need symbols like these, check out the fonts. You can even open the font in a font-editing program like Fontographer and customize it. Typefaces are PIXymbols Hotel and PIXymbols Travel.*

*Instant logos!*
*Typefaces are Jimbo Standard Black Expanded,*
*Isadora (script), PIXymbols Travel (pictograph).*

. . . . . . . . . . . . . . . . . . . . . . . . . . . . . . . . . . . . . . . . . . . . . . . . . . . .

# Picture fonts

Picture fonts, where each character is a little picture, can be used in oh so many ways. Similar to dingbats, you can use them as bullets. Or instead of a dotted or dashed line, try a line made of a picture font character or a combination of characters. Use them as borders, as clip art, as custom art. You can make them very small, add space between them, or even change their color easily.

Picture fonts are great for quick, easy, and inexpensive logos. You can enlarge a picture character to the maximum size in your program, sometimes as large as 18 inches. You can change their color, condense or expand them, kern them, and build them right into the text of the logo. If you know how to use a program like Fontographer from FontLab, you can customize the character and still use it as easily as you would the letter A.

*The character shown on the left, from the picture font Printers Ornaments M, had the right feel but slightly the wrong look for the intended logo. I opened the font in Fontographer and just moved a few points to give the character more female lines, as shown on the right. The other face is Eurostile.*

*These fonts are so much fun to collect and use everywhere. Drop pictures into memos to your boss, love letters, signs, business cards, t-shirts— have fun! Typefaces are MiniPics Lil Ancients, Birds, and MiniPics Doohickies Too.*

*You can create interesting borders out of many picture fonts. Typeface is MiniPics Doohickies Too.*

## Rebus stories

And when you run out of things to do, gather your kids, a couple of picture and pi fonts, and create a rebus story. Although the stories are generally pretty silly, I guarantee the process will make you laugh, and that's a valuable thing.

ONCE upon a time there was a little 🏃 who had a 🐕 named Fido. One ☀ day the 🐕 chased a 🐈. This 🐈 had just caught a 🐁. The cat's friend was having a birthday party with a 🎂 and the 🐈 was bringing this dead 🐁 as a birthday present. Before the 🐈 could get to the 🏠 for the party, the 🐕 started chasing him. A little 🐵 saw the predicament and jumped in his new red 🚗 and sped off to get his friend the 🐦 who really couldn't do anything to help and so the 🐕 ate the 🐈 who had killed the 🐁 on this ☀ day and that was that.

*Typeface is Hansel, which includes the letters and the pictures.*

## Note!

When you print picture and pi fonts, check your Print dialog box and see if you have a button that says, "Use Symbol font for special characters." If you do, *un*check this button or you will print the wrong symbols!

# Don't be a Wimp!

ype has just recently become a household item. The media tells us that people are reading less and less, yet type is becoming more and more important. How many typefaces could you name ten years ago? How many do you now have on your computer? How many billboards, book covers, t-shirts, and ice cream containers do you now look at and wonder what the typeface is?

A result of this increased awareness of typography is increased power and strength of printed words. Everyone is more conscious of the words—not just what they say, but how they are presented. Type is art, but art with a clear purpose. The next chapter talks about evocative typography, and about choosing typefaces that reinforce your message. But in this short chapter I simply want to exhort you to take full advantage of this new typographic consciousness. It is so easy to make your pages alive, exciting, provocative—but never forget that your purpose is to communicate.

## Extremes

Don't be afraid to go to extremes. Find ways to use type extremely large or extremely small, at least in proportion to the piece. I recently received a letter with the name and address of the sender in some really funky type at least two inches tall. It had an incredible impact—full of chutzpah and creativity. In phone book advertising, newspaper ads, brochures, flyers, in many, many places, try using extraordinarily large type. A good contrast would be to have the body of the piece in a decently small size, say 10 point. Don't think that because the heading is so large that the rest of the type has to be larger than average also—no no! It is specifically that strong contrast between the large and the small that makes the piece so effective.

. . . . . . . . . . . . . . . . . . . . . . . . . . . . . . . . . . . . . . . . . . . . . .

# White space

It's okay to have white space, empty space on your page that is not filled with text or graphics or anything but clean empty space. It's okay. You can do it. Your type will love it. When you find type treatments that appeal to you, take a moment to see where that designer let the white space be. Chances are there is a fair amount of it. Look through this book at all the white space. Look through other books and see how much white space they have, and be conscious of your reaction to the ones that have very little. Be brave enough to let the empty space just sit there. It's okay.

## Odd typefAces

There are so many wonderfully offbeat typefaces available—oh my my my! Once you get up the nerve to use them, you'll find they are appropriate in many more ways that you might have first thought. If you're a little shy, start off using them on projects for which you don't have clients, such as postcards to friends, invitations to your daughter's birthday party, flyers for your lost dog, the family chore list, your Christmas letter, or as graphic text on your web page. Once the odd typefaces become part of your repertoire, sneak them into a memo to your boss—just one word for now:

## Memo    MEMO    Memo    MeMo

She'll hardly notice. Start *infiltrating* it around the office—notices in the lunchroom, minutes to *the meetings*, instructions *in the restrooms*. It is a sad fact of human existence that we tend to fear what we don't know, so make your favorite wild font a local, familiar face. Everyone will become friends and then you can introduce it to your stationery and business cards. Ha!

# Typographic Choices

In which we explore typefaces that evoke a response from the reader, tips on choosing a typeface, trends in type, and desktop publishing pitfalls.

# You cannot *not*
# communicate. Paul Watzlawick

# Evocative Typography

Evocative typography refers to a choice of typeface that reinforces the message of the words, type that evokes a desired response. Designers have always been very careful about their choice of type, and I know you have been through that process many times. You have a definite idea of which faces would be appropriate for different projects. You wouldn't make a Garage Sale sign in German blackletter. You wouldn't do a brochure for fire safety in a grungy, deconstructive font that's hard to read (or set the directions in all caps).

What I want to accomplish with this chapter, though, is to encourage you to push the concept of evocative typography even further than you have been, and also to take a closer look at what you are evoking. If the first thing that comes to mind for a Japanese tea garden festival is a typeface made out of little pagodas, toss it. Corny and overused. Consider what symbolizes the festival— grace, beauty, tradition? Perhaps try a lovely oldstyle with graceful curves, set large so you can enjoy its beauty. Do some research, discover that the most popular typeface in Japan for many years was Baskerville, a transitional oldstyle— try that. Maybe you need to do a flyer for the children's museum. Your first thought is to use a hand-scrawled typeface with backwards characters. If the flyer is for kids, try using real letters instead of cute lettering that reinforces backwards letters. Try New Century Schoolbook, which was designed for children's books, or a clean sans serif that emulates the way children write their alphabet. You can always use picture fonts to add playful illustrations all over the page.

Next time you need to decide on a typeface that reinforces the text, think it through carefully. Don't always go with your first idea. Since we are on computers, it is so easy to play with all of our options, to change faces with the click of a button. Typefaces are cheap now—invest in a variety! Remember, you can never have too much money, too much RAM, or too many fonts.

## Easy choices

Some choices will be very easy, some you will have to think about. The ones below are easy—circle the typeface that would probably communicate the message best for each of these examples:

**Lost Shih-Tzu Puppy!**    *Fette Fraktur*

*Lost Shih-Tzu Puppy*    *Carpenter*

**Lost Shih-Tzu Puppy!**    *Myriad Pro Black*

---

TOULOUSE-LAUTREC SHOW OPENS FRIDAY    *Pierre Bonnard*

TOULOUSE-LAUTREC SHOW
OPENS FRIDAY    *Karton*

Toulouse-Lautrec Show Opens    *Prestige Elite*

---

'62 WILLYS PICKUP
FOR SALE    *Gladys*

**'62 Willys Pickup For Sale**    *Franklin
Gothic Roman*

*'62 Willys Pickup For Sale*    *Emily Austin*

## More difficult choices

Many of the choices you will have to make are not so easy (unless you only have six fonts on your computer). Push your creative process, think about what you really mean, play with visual puns, make people think about what they read.

*Work Hard.*
**There is no shortcut.**

*I'll bet these type choices bother you. I'll bet you think "Work Hard" should be the phrase in big, solid, bold type. Well, y'see, it all depends on your point of view and what you want to express.*

*In my life, this is how I see it: Ya work hard.* **THERE IS NO SHORTCUT** *(please excuse the all caps). That's the way it is—it's a fact of life that you work hard. What was difficult to get through my teenagers' heads is that* **there is no shortcut.**

*Typefaces are Isadora and Antique Olive Nord.*

❶ I Quit.

❷ **I Quit.**

❸ I Quit.

❹ *I Quit.*

*So how would you quit? It might depend on the job and the circumstances, of course. Maybe one day you would quit in* ❶ *Marie Luise and another day you would quit in* ❷ *Clarendon. Maybe your boss drives you to quit in* ❸ *Chicken. I can tell you that most any day I would quit in* ❹ *Shelley Volante, with a sassy smile on my face and my fingers toodle-ooing goodbye. See ya later, alligator!*

# Think it through

If you have something important to say and you want to reinforce the message with typography, think it through very carefully. There is a place for platitudes. Sometimes the most obvious solution is the best, just as the trite phrase, "like looking for a needle in a haystack" is very clear—a reader can make no mistake about what you mean. All of our tired phrases have a reason for being true—we get it. We get the point. We see the connection. We understand the analogy. So there is also a place in typography for the old saws.

But don't neglect the beauty of a new turn of phrase, a new way of expressing an old thought, a new twist on a tired idea. Sometimes it will behoove you to probe a little deeper, think about the project, and write down the various ideas you are trying to project. Look at your type choices carefully—the more you work with type, the more you will become conscious of the details that project an image.

It is not just the details of the typeface that create a response, it is how you use it. Say you choose a tall, narrow modern to project a sophisticated, highbrow appearance to the ad for your small store. Emphasize that tall and narrow with a strong flush right or left with narrow line lengths, perhaps lots of linespace, maybe a trendy ornament or two.

Keep a file of graphic design pieces that created a strong response in you—good or bad. Take a few moments to put into words how an appropriate response from the reader was created: note the details, the alignments, the white space, and the combination of typefaces. In pieces that evoked an inappropriate response (different from what you think they wanted), figure out where the contradictions are—the typeface, the linespace, the angles, or other details? *The more you are able to see and put these things into words, the more control and power you have in designing your own work.*

Keep your eyes open, and be conscious!

# Choose a Typeface

## WHAT TYPEFACE SHALL I USE? THE GODS REFUSE TO ANSWER. THEY REFUSE BECAUSE THEY DO NOT KNOW.
W. A. Dwiggins

Dwiggins' cry to the gods is one with which we are all familiar. Even though there are more than 50,000 typefaces available to us, finding the perfect font for a particular job can be a stressful task. Or more likely it is *because* we have 50,000 fonts to choose from that the task often appears monumental. There are steps you can take, though, to narrow the selection down to a handful of appropriate choices.

## Remember those categories of type?

First of all, remember those general categories of type you read about in the beginning of this book? And remember the sections on readability and legibility? Understanding those categories and concepts is important in helping narrow your choices, so let's review them.

**Oldstyle** faces have slanted serifs, gradual thick-to-thin strokes, and a slanted stress (the O appears tilted). The original oldstyle faces were created for books, so they are eminently readable.

**Modern** faces have thin, horizontal serifs, radical thick-to-thin strokes, and a vertical stress (the O does not appear to tilt). If there is more than a paragraph or two of a modern face, the strong thick/thin contrast in the letterforms creates a "dazzling" effect that makes modern typefaces less than perfectly readable. The more pronounced the contrast in the stroke, the less readable in extended text.

**Slab serif** faces have thick, horizontal serifs, little or no thick/thin transition in the strokes, and a vertical stress (the O does not appear to tilt). If the slab serif is not too heavy, it can make a very sturdy and solid readable face.

• • • • • • • • • • • • • • • • • • • • • • • • • • • • • • • • • • • • • • • • • • • • • • •

**Sans serif** faces have no serifs, and almost all sans serifs have monoweight strokes (no thick/thin contrast at all). The absence of serifs and the monoweight strokes make sans serifs slightly *less readable* than oldstyles, but because they have such clearly defined letterforms without the addition of little diddlies like serifs, this style is actually *more legible* than serif faces in short bursts of text.

Remember, on a computer monitor, sans serif can be easier to read because there are fewer fine details, like serifs, that get lost or clunky on the screen. Just be sure to make the line lengths shorter and stay away from heavy weights when setting lots of text.

You probably need no review on what defines a typeface as **script, decorative,** or **fringe**—they're pretty self-explanatory.

And do you also remember reading about **readability** and **legibility?** The more distinctive features, the *less* readable it is, the less suitable for long blocks of text. The oldstyle category and the light weights of slab serifs are the *most* "invisible" and subsequently the most *readable*. Sans serifs tend to be more *legible* because they have clean, straightforward letterforms.

## Questions about your project

To narrow the choices of faces for a printed project, here are questions to ask yourself. The questions are not ranked in order of importance—each one is a critical consideration.

>  **What is your output printer resolution:**
>  Low (72–144 dots per inch; this would have to be a very old printer),
>  Medium (300–600 dpi), or
>  High-resolution imagesetter (1270–2540 dpi)?
>  Are you going straight through a fax machine
>  (consider it low resolution)?
>
>  **What will be the final reproduction method:**
>  Copy machine, quick press, high-quality press?
>
>  **On what kind of paper will you be reproducing the project:**
>  Newsprint, cheap bond, textured stock, glossy stock, fax paper?

. . . . . . . . . . . . . . . . . . . . . . . . . . . . . . . . . . . . . . . . . . . . . . .

## Quality

The common thread between these questions is *quality*—the quality of type onscreen, the quality of the type itself that comes out of the printer, the quality of the reproduction method, and the quality of the paper. If each of these variables is on the high end, then you can use any typeface you choose as far as technical reproduction is concerned. If any of these variables is on the low end (or on textured paper, even though it's high quality), you need to be more selective to make sure your type will reproduce well.

## Less than very high quality

- Type from a lower resolution printer or some cheap color printers cannot retain subtle design characteristics, such as very fine lines or delicate serifs.

- A copy machine or a fax machine also loses some of the fine details in the reproduction process.

- Inexpensive paper, especially newsprint, absorbs ink and loses even more, sometimes to the point of filling in the counters (those spaces inside letters like **e** or **d**).

**For any of the poorer conditions,** choose a typeface that has sturdy serifs, no fine lines, and a larger x-height with open counters, such as those shown below. Most sans serifs will hold up very well under any conditions, and are the easiest to read onscreen due to their simplicity of form. Also look through font catalogs for typefaces with these characteristics.

## **Clarendon Plain or** Clarendon Light
## *New Century Schoolbook*
## **Bookman**
## Memphis

*All of these faces have solid strokes and serifs that*
*will not fall apart under difficult printing conditions.*

. . . . . . . . . . . . . . . . . . . . . . . . . . . . . . . . . . . . . . . . . . . . . . . . . . . .

# Is there an extensive amount of text to read?

If you have an extended amount of text, as in a lengthy newsletter, an annual report, or a book, you need a body typeface with maximum readability (see Chapter 2). Under the best printing conditions (high-resolution output, smooth paper, and a good printing press), try a classic oldstyle for best readability. You are reading Adobe Caslon Pro Regular right now, which is a classic oldstyle.

Under the worst printing conditions, try a typeface in the slab serif category. It will be extremely readable but will not fall apart in the reproduction process.

This typeface (in the modern category) would give you a headache in a long body of text. It's too extreme in many ways. In fact, don't you find it difficult to read even in this short bit? Great for headlines:

# Hats off to you!

This typeface will hold up well even under the worst conditions, is clean and orderly, has a business-like presentation, and would be readable in extensive text (not quite as readable as an oldstyle face). This is Clarendon Light, a slab serif. **It also comes in this Clarendon Plain which is a little heavier, and this Clarendon Bold for a great and sturdy impression.**

*Compare reading these two samples, plus the two paragraphs above the samples. Do you get a feeling for which are easiest to read? Once you are conscious of it, the details that make a typeface readable become obvious. Typefaces are Bodoni Poster Compressed on the left, Clarendon family on the right.*

. . . . . . . . . . . . . . . . . . . . . . . . . . . . . . . . . . . . . . . . . . . . .

# Are you cramped for space, or do you need to fill space?

You've probably noticed that different typefaces take up different amounts of space, even at the same point size (see page 16 on the anatomy of type). The most critical factor for this difference is the width of the characters. The type family Times has an average x-height, but the characters are slightly condensed to fit more on the page. Other faces, such as Garamond, are more round and open and fill a page easily. Plus, if a typeface is open, it also likes to have extra line spacing and wider margins to complement its spaciousness, which you can take advantage of to further fill the space.

You'll find differences even between typefaces that have the same family name but have been created by different font vendors, as in the example below!

There are entire books of type which display paragraphs of text set in a wide variety of fonts. By comparing the paragraphs you can see which fonts can fit more text in a given space at a given size. Check your local public library or college library for type books.

*13-pica line*

The loss of the state of innocence in which Baskerville looks like Bembo, and Helvetica is indistinguishable from Universe, has the compensating advantage that we become more aware of the tiny details and the 'subtle allure' which go to make up the best faces.

*Sebastian Carter*

Adobe Garamond Pro Regular  10.5/13

*13-pica line*

The loss of the state of innocence in which Baskerville looks like Bembo, and Helvetica is indistinguishable from Universe, has the compensating advantage that we become more aware of the tiny details and the 'subtle allure' which go to make up the best faces.

Sebastian Carter

ITC Garamond Book  10.5/13

*Even though the two paragraphs above are both set in Garamond at the same point size, the Adobe Pro version takes up less space than the ITC version. You can imagine how this could change your entire newsletter or novel!*

. . . . . . . . . . . . . . . . . . . . . . . . . . . . . . . . . . . . . . . . . . . . . . . . . . . . . . . . . . . . .

# Is the purpose of the piece rather sedate, or can the text be a little playful?

Sometimes even when there is a fair amount of text, as in a brochure, you don't want or really need an invisible typeface. There are many typefaces that are certainly readable enough for short text, but also distinctive enough to create a look that emphasizes your message. Realize you are making a choice between ideal readability and an impression, and get as playful as you like as long as you can justify your choice.

## A casual look versus a serious look

❶ I'm sure you already have a sense of which typefaces appear more casual and informal than others, but noticing exactly what kinds of features create that look gives you more strength behind your choices.

❷ Casual faces tend to be more distinctive; their features often have quirks. Rounded, soft edges make it more comfortable; serifs that curve or branch off at odd angles give it a friendly twitch. Faces that resemble handlettering or handwriting of course have a casual feel. These quirky or softened features are comparable to wearing red cowboy boots or sneakers—they create a distinctly casual impression no matter what the words themselves say.

❸ The typefaces with a more professional or serious and stable look are the "invisible" faces I mentioned in the readability chapter, the ones that simply communicate clearly with no quirks. These are the gray suits of typography, the bastions of respectability, the guys in the mold.

*So which of the three paragraphs above is the gray suit, which is the evening gown, and which is the t-shirt?*

*Typefaces are Bernhard Modern, Improv, and Caslon Pro Regular.*

. . . . . . . . . . . . . . . . . . . . . . . . . . . . . . . . . . . . . . . . . . . . . . .

# Is the project to be skimmed or really read?

In a job like a catalog or parts list where the reader will primarily be skimming headlines to find the text they want to read, keep in mind that sans serif faces are more legible, meaning the separate character forms are more easily distinguished at a quick glance (as long as they are not set in all caps!). You are also more likely to find condensed versions of sans serif faces, which are often necessary in the kind of piece where you're trying to get a lot of information onto the pages. And a sans serif will hold up well under the often less-than-ideal printing conditions of many catalogs or parts lists.

If the sans serif catalog headlines are meant to lead readers into *paragraphs* of text, consider using a serif face for the paragraphs, both for maximum readability and for visual contrast.

**HEADS**
**Storage for the mind.**
**Available in many sizes**
**and preferences.**

**SHOULDERS**
**Come in broad, narrow,**
**strong enough to carry**
**the worries of the world.**

**KNEES**
**Choose from knobby,**
**knock, bad, or weak.**

**TOES**
**Order ten at a time for**
**the most comfortable fit.**

**EYES**
**Wide range of colors.**
**Can choose an attitude**
**to go along with.**

**EARS**
**Everything from small**
**and sweet to large and**
**winglike.**

**WAISTLINES**
**Whatever you order,**
**keep an eye on it as it**
**tends to disappear as**
**you get older.**

**Heads**
Storage for the mind.
Available in many sizes
and preferences.

**Shoulders**
Come in broad, narrow,
strong enough to carry
the worries of the world.

**Knees**
Choose from knobby,
knock, bad, or weak.

**Toes**
Order ten at a time for
the most comfortable fit.

**Eyes**
Wide range of colors.
Can choose an attitude
to go along with.

**Ears**
Everything from small and
sweet to large and winglike.

**Waistlines**
Whatever you order,
keep an eye on it as
it tends to disappear
as you get older.

*So what makes the second list easier to read, and makes the heads easier to scan?*

- *Upper- and lowercase instead of all caps.*

- *Extra space above each head.*

- *Contrast with the body copy.*

- *Sans serif for heads (Formata Bold), serif for body copy (Garamond).*

# Evocative typography

Notice these questions don't even address the subject of whether a particular typeface suits your job emotionally; that is, whether the look-and-feel of the face itself reinforces your message. I do hope you read Chapter 29 on "Evocative Typography" for some suggestions on this most interesting of typographic questions.

Within the limits of your reproduction process, push your creativity here. Experiment with new and different faces, faces you might not have considered at first. Don't analyze them—get your gut reaction. Keep your eyes open for what others have done, consciously clip examples of unusual type choices and file them for later inspiration. You'll be surprised at what can work!

# DECORATIVE AND FRINGE FONTS

There are so many wonderful and wild typefaces now, with more being created every day. Obviously, these intriguing fonts are for special occasions, but what occasions! Just be careful not to overdose your reader with too much of a special face—its strong impact will be diluted. Rather than use a uniquely creative face for all the headlines in your newsletter, save it for one very special article. The contrast between the stable headlines and the wild one will give your special article more impact.

*Headline typeface is Erosive.*

. . . . . . . . . . . . . . . . . . . . . . . . . . . . . . . . . . . . . . . . . . . . . . . . .

# An exercise and method

I recommend you go to the web sites of the font vendors listed in Appendix B of this book. If they provide a printed catalog, request it. Spend a few minutes looking carefully at many faces on the web site or in the catalog and try to place each one into one of the general categories of type. Once you have found its basic place (many will not fit neatly into a category—that's okay, just get as close as possible), then make some judgments. Does it have distinctive features or is it invisible? Does it wear red cowboy boots or a gray suit? Does the face have fine, delicate features that might not hold up through a fax machine, a copier, or on textured or cheap paper? Or does it have sturdy features that can go through the wash?

## Analyze your project

❦ Know your output method and final reproduction process, and narrow your choices down to appropriate faces that will retain their design qualities. (Reread, if necessary, Chapters 2 and 3 on readability and legibility.)

❦ Decide on the look you want to convey, then narrow your choices to the distinctive or the invisible (or a combination that is exciting and still readable).

❦ If you use more than one face, make sure the fonts are decidedly different from each other. If you have chosen a beautiful oldstyle for the body text, try a bold sans serif for headlines. (If you haven't yet, you might want to read another book of mine, *The Non-Designer's Design Book*. The second half of the book focuses on the specific issue of combining typefaces.)

❦ Don't be afraid to use wild fonts where they are appropriate, and remember they are most effective (as is any rich item) when used sparingly—the richer, the more powerful. But don't be a wimp!

THE GOOD THING IS THAT
WE HAVE SO MANY FONTS.
THE BAD THING IS THAT
WE HAVE SO MANY FONTS.

# Telltale Signs of *Desktop Publishing*

Desktop publishing has matured from the classic ransom notes we were inundated with in the mid-1980s. People have become much more visually aware and informed about the professional way to set their own type and design their own pages. But telltale signs of do-it-yourself desktop publishing still creep into even the most professional work. Some of these signs are a result of not knowing the software well enough to control certain features, and some are simply evidence of using convenient features that really shouldn't even be options—or, in some cases, defaults—on the computer.

Give yourself three penalty points for each of the following telltale signs that you perpetrate. If you score three or above, you lose.

· · · · · · · · · · · · · · · · · · · · · · · · · · · · · · · · · · · · · · · · · · · · · · · · · · · · · · · · · ·

# 1. Helvetica

Type has trends, just like hair styles and clothing and eyeglasses and architecture. **Helvetica** was the most popular typeface in the world in the 1960s, and in the '70s it was a way of life. By the '80s Helvetica was becoming as passé as beehive hairdos and then it appeared in the Macintosh font menu and then in the PC font menu under the name **Arial.** Just as a beehive hairdo creates a certain look, Helvetica creates a certain look. A dated look. A '70s look. Just because it's on your computer doesn't mean you have to use it. The greatest thing you could do for your publications is to invest in another sans serif face, one with a strong, bold black version in its family. As with all trends, Helvetica will someday be back in style—in about two hundred years.

## This is Helvetica — groovy, man.

Try anything else: Trade Gothic, **Formata, Antique Olive,** Eurostile!

# 2. Straight quotes

It is amazing that after all these years people are still typing straight quotes. Learn the keystrokes to type real quotes, and in every application you use, take advantage of the feature that types them for you automatically (read your manual!). But don't type curly quotes when you need inch and foot marks (in fact, use prime marks; remember Chapter 4)! And don't type an opening quote at the beginning of a word that really needs an apostrophe! And put the quotation marks and apostrophes in the right places!

"Can you believe that dog stands 7'3" tall? Its huge!"

"Can you believe that dog stands 7'3" tall? It's huge!"

*Notice the prime marks for the numbers, and the quotation marks are hanging!*

. . . . . . . . . . . . . . . . . . . . . . . . . . . . . . . . . . . . . . . . . . . . . . . . . .

# 3. Double returns

Hitting the Return or Enter key twice between paragraphs or after headlines separates the text with big, awkward gaps. Double Returns also make it possible to end up with a blank line at the top of a column.

Learn to use the feature to set "Paragraph space after" and "Paragraph space before." It's in every word processor and page layout application. With that feature you can determine exactly the amount of space you want between paragraphs, after headlines, above subheads—an elegant space that tells the reader a new paragraph has begun without physically separating the text so much.

Notice the difference between these three paragraphs and the rest of the paragraphs in the book—wouldn't you agree that the gap appears unnecessarily large?

# 4. Two spaces after punctuation

I know, I know—if you are still typing two spaces after periods it is probably because you firmly believe it looks better that way.   If all the work you create is for yourself, go ahead and continue to type two spaces. But you would be doing your clients a disservice to set *their* type with two spaces after periods because by now most people have become visually astute enough to notice the unsightly gaps created by that double space. Publications typed with two spaces have an unprofessional appearance, whether you agree with it or not, and your work will be ridiculed. Open any novel on your shelf—see any double spaces?   Did you read that novel and complain to yourself that you couldn't tell where the sentences ended?   The high-quality type you are using, with its proportional widths and kerning pairs that tuck the letters so close together, does not need two spaces to separate sentences.   Squint at this paragraph—notice any holes?

· · · · · · · · · · · · · · · · · · · · · · · · · · · · · · · · · · · · · · · · · · · · · · · · · · · ·

# 5. Gray boxes behind text

Just because you *can* make gray boxes doesn't mean that you have to. Beginners often use gray boxes to make important parts of the text stand out because they don't have other ideas about how to make type a focal point, or at least make it a little more important than average. Besides screaming "amateur," type on that dotted, gray background is difficult to read. (Even worse are gray boxes with rounded corners. I know you have a tool for making rounded corner boxes. So.)

If you want to make a portion of the text stand out, try something else: a dramatic headline font, reverse bold heads, heavy rules (lines) above and below the article, extra space around the type. Keep your eyes open and see what others do—copy those ideas!

> *Warning:*
> Do not touch the red knob while cleaning this machine or you will detonate the blasting cap and the machine will explode.

*Besides looking plain ol' dumb, the lack of contrast between the gray background and the words also makes the text difficult to read.*

# Warning!

Do not touch the red knob while cleaning this machine or you will detonate the blasting cap and the machine will explode.

*White space, heavy and thin rules, bold typeface—oh, so many ways to call attention to text without using gray boxes.*

. . . . . . . . . . . . . . . . . . . . . . . . . . . . . . . . . . . . . . . . . . . . . . . . . . . . .

# 6. Centered layouts

Centered type creates a stable, sedate, formal look because it is so symmetrical and balanced. It can also create a deadly dull look. New designers center type because it is a very safe thing to do. If you center the page because you *want* a more formal look, that's one thing. But if you center the page because you simply haven't thought about it, or because you are afraid of uncentering it, that's another thing. As you flip through any magazine, stop at the layouts that interest you. Most of the pages and ads that have a strong, dynamic feeling are not centered. An invisible line connects the elements in a flush left or flush right alignment, and the strength of that line gives strength to the entire page.

If you are going to center, then do it with gusto. Don't try to make all the lines similar lengths; instead, show off the fact that it's centered. And if you're going to center, center *everything*—don't stick something in the left-hand corner just to fill the corner. Corners don't mind being empty.

I think and think for
months and years. Ninety-
nine times, the conclusion
is false. The hundredth
time I am right.

*Albert Einstein*

I think and think
for months
and years.
Ninety-nine times,
the conclusion is false.
**The hundredth time
I am right.**

*Albert Einstein*

*Mmm, nice and boring. And the
typography in no way reinforces
the message of the text.*

*What did I do
to this centered arrangement
to make it a bit more
dynamic?
Name five things.*

*Typeface is Obelisk Light, Bold,
and Italic.*

## 7. Borders around everything

One border around a page often indicates a beginner who feels unsafe with type that is uncontained. The more boxes of type with borders around them, the more insecure the designer. I know, it feels safer to box it in; it gives the type a place to *be*, without just floating in the space. But y'know what? It's okay to let it be. Really. That white space (the "empty" space) is itself a border—it encloses the type, yet lets it breathe; it defines the edges, yet maintains a freedom.

## 8. Half-inch indents

Yes, I know your typing teacher taught you to indent five spaces or one-half inch, but that's a very old habit left over from typewriters. Typically on a typewriter a person was typing all the way across the page, and the type was relatively large.

A standard typographic indent is one em space, which is a space as wide as the point size of the type. In 10-point type, an em space is 10 points wide; in 36-point type, an em space is 36 points wide. This is roughly equivalent to *two* spaces, not five. Especially when your type is in columns, a half-inch indent is way out of proportion.

## 9. Hyphens or asterisks for bullets

- Using hyphens or asterisks as bullets is a typewriter habit, and it looks dumb in professional type.

* The round dot bullet (•, type Option 8) is a little better, but experiment with more interesting bullets.

- You can get strong little squares or triangles out of Zapf Dingbats, or play with other picture fonts. Make them smaller and use the baseline shift feature to raise them off the baseline (read the manual!).

* It's amazing how this little touch can add more sophistication to a piece. See Chapter 26.

## 10. Outlined shadowed type

Type that has been outlined and shadowed automatically by the computer still shows up, and in the most surprising places (like book covers, billboards, and annual reports). Don't do it. If you're just starting to use your computer, I know the temptation is great because with the click of a button you can make your type fancy. And that's the impression it gives—someone trying to make their type look fancy because they don't know what else to do with it. When you let the computer add a shadow with the click of a button, you have no control over where the shadow goes or how thick it is, and most often it just looks cluttered and junky because of all the different parts of the letters in various layers. It creates an especially bad effect if the type is a script face.

Again, look around, try to put into words what other people have done to make their type stand out without resorting to using outlines and shadows.

*Meet the host!*

## 11. Twelve-point type and auto leading

Just because the default is 12-point type with auto leading doesn't mean you have to use it. For most typefaces, 12-point is a tiny bit too large for body copy. Take a paragraph of 12-point text and set the same paragraph in 10, 11, or perhaps 10.5 point. Compare the two printed pieces; notice which one gives you a more professional, sophisticated impression. Add an extra 1 or 1.5 points of linespace (leading). Compare them again. What do you think?

. . . . . . . . . . . . . . . . . . . . . . . . . . . . . . . . . . . . . . . . . . . . . . . . . . .

# 12. Underlines in print

This is a law: **never use the underline feature.** An underline in print means one thing: *italicize* this word. I know you were taught to underline titles of books, but that's because the typewriter (or your teacher) couldn't set italics. And <u>*underlining italic text*</u> is one of the most redundant things you can do in life. I know you sometimes underlined to emphasize a headline or a word, but that's because you didn't know how to make the type bolder or bigger or a different face. Now you know. Now you have no excuse.

Drawing a rule ("rule" means line) under text is very different from hitting the underline keystroke. When you draw a rule you have control over how thick it is, how long it is, and how far below the type it sits. But when you tell your computer to underline, the line bumps into the letters, obscures the descenders, is a clunky thickness, and looks dumb.

Some layout applications, such as Adobe InDesign, let you determine how thick a computer underline is, how far away from the text it is, what kind of line it is (dotted, double, etc.), what color the line should be, and if there is a gap in the line, what color the gap should be. Essentially, this feature lets you create a rule *under selected characters,* as opposed to the paragraph rule feature, which sets a line of your choice under or above the first or last line of a paragraph.

# 13. All caps

All caps are more difficult to read. That's just a fact: we recognize a word not only by its letters, but by the shape of the whole word. When text is in all caps, every word has the same shape so we have to go back to reading letter by letter.

All caps are fine sometimes, when you *consciously* choose to accept their lower readability because you need the look of all caps. But when you're setting headlines, subheads, lists in a parts directory, catalog entries, or other items that need to be skimmed and absorbed quickly, all are read more easily and quickly if they are in lowercase. If you use all caps because you want the words to stand out, or because it makes them appear larger and you think it's easier to read, THINK AGAIN. Find an alternate solution, such as **bold lowercase,** more space surrounding the text, **a different typeface,** <u>a rule beneath,</u> behind, or above the text.

And of course no one reading this book would ever put a font like Zapfino or Zapf Chancery in all caps. And outlined and shadowed. Score fifty-one points for yourself if you do. The capital letters in script faces are always more elaborate because they are meant as swash characters to introduce a word. When you set these froufrou letters in all caps, they bump into each other, overlap where they shouldn't, fit poorly together, and generally look stupid. Add the outline and shadow and you have the worst possible typography on earth, worse than any grunge type you may cringe at.

## Your score?

If you scored above three points, don't worry. Creating professional-level type is mainly a matter of becoming more aware of details. It usually doesn't take any more time to do it "right," and it is certainly not difficult to gain control over these details. If you scored less than three, then congratulations, and consider it your obligation to gently teach others the things you know.

I base my fashion taste on what doesn't itch.

*Trends in Type*
*by John Tollett*

Fifteen years ago, how many typesetters and typographic designers did you know on a first-name basis? And how many do you know today? I'm willing to bet my last, crumpled, 1980s vintage sheet of press type that *most* of the people you know have a better type selection at their fingertips than many professional typographers used to have in their shops. I'll do better than that. I'll bet my treasured, white-handled, tooth-marked x-acto knife that within the past hour or so, you've made a life-or-Helvetica decision.

Back when I was using that x-acto knife's handle to burnish down that sheet of press type, if someone had asked me to bring them up to date on current type trends, I would have noted the revival of some dated faces like Cheltenham, or the popularity of extra-tight letter spacing in headlines. They would have looked at me and smirked, "Golly, I'm *so* impressed! Tell me [yawn] more."

But that was then and this is now. The technology of desktop and web publishing has transformed the old graphics neighborhood into a much more exciting, innovative, and creative world. And that's why identifying trends is difficult… there's so much happening on such a steep curve of change that current trends don't have the opportunities that our ancestor trends had. But, hey, this is the digital era and if you want to make it as a trend, you're going to have to really wow us with your stuff.

For the sake of this discussion, let's say that *trends in type* refers to both *font design* (the look and feel of the individual characters of a font) and to *typographic design* (using type as the major visual element in layout and design). This makes a huge category, but I nominate the following six entries as the most obvious candidates for trendom.

. . . . . . . . . . . . . . . . . . . . . . . . . . . . . . . . . . . . . . . . . . . . . . . . . .

# 1. MOST CONTROVERSIAL

## TREND: UGLY TYPE, LAWLESS DESIGN

This one really rocked the boat. If you haven't seen it, you've been spending too much time at the Helvetica User Group meetings. Some people think these ugly fonts are a fad that has started to fade. But if you look around, you'll realize that grunge type and lawless design is not only everywhere, it's so common that it doesn't shock us like it used to. Ugly fonts are not only outrageous by traditional standards, sometimes they range between barely legible and you-gotta-be-kidding-if-you-think-I-can-read-this. But g    u    e    s    s what else they are? They're interesting.

Designers who are trying to get your attention, who are trying to convey a feeling with type, are using ugly fonts and ugly design. Ugly design abandons most things that are familiar to us, such as consistent leading, symmetrical columns, reasonable contrast between words and Background, in favor of lines of type crashing into each other, columns of type crashing into each other, columns of type on top of each other, words bleeding off the page and anything else that would terminate your employment in most places. There are some traditionalists who are getting close to marching through the streets with torches and pitchforks to round up grunge design before it destroys our typographic village. Some aren't worried at all because it's laughable that such a ridiculous thing could have much influence. Uh oh. Look around you. mtv. espn. National magazines, national advertisers... everyone is feeling the graphic influence of grunge. Like trends in fashion, designers take elements of what's happening in the most extreme cases and use them in more conservative ways. You'll

• • • • • • • • • • • • • • • • • • • • • • • • • • • • • • • • • • • • •

see ugly fonts used in traditional layouts. I've used

some very stranGe fonts for some very conservative clients
(a community college, a banK, and a magazine
for CAD engineers). Some designers
prefer using traditional, classical typefaces in a grun-
ge-inspired layout. Some do both. You Don't have to plunge into
grunge, but it's really fun to
get your feet wet.

· · · · · · · · · · · · · · · · · · · · · · · · · · · · · · · · · · · · · · · · · · · · · · · · · · · · · · · ·

# 2. Most Amazing Trend: Special Effects Type

The first time I saw a designer stretching and squeezing type on a computer monitor, I knew my graphic life was going to change, but little did I know how magical changes those changes would be.

Some of the things you can do with type today aren't new. Dazzling effects were being created before desktop publishing, but mainly by those lucky enough to have giant budgets and lengthy production schedules. Most of us flipped through the design annuals of yesteryear and wondered how this was done or what genius did that? Who has that much time or budget? Fortunately, there was a digital daybreak on the horizon emblazoned with the motto: New Ballgame, Amigo!

Tired of flat type just lying there, staring at you? With software and software plug-ins available today you can transform your headline into a piece of art, or at least an eye-stopping dynamic graphic. You can render a word or a sentence in 3D, rotate it, render it in color, and specify what direction the light is coming from and what color the light is. Change the color of the ambient light and map a texture to the surface of the type. Bevel the edge of the type. Create a soft drop shadow that blends into the background color. Twirl, zig, zag, ripple, shatter, or vector warp your type. Shade the inside of the type with blends of color. You can do all this at your desktop in less time than it used to take you to find the phone number of some master handlettering expert.

The software tools for creating special effects are getting more powerful, more affordable, and easier to use, so this is a trend that is just becoming a way of life. The only designers jumping off this bandwagon are ones who are looking for the next big whatever. The next time one of these techniques jumps off the page at you, say hello to a trend.

# 3. Most Beautiful Trend: Rendered Type

I've separated this category from the previous one because this is really a combination of illustration, animation, and typography. These typographic examples *really* used to be out of reach. Before desktop graphics, how often were you going to hire photographers, illustrators, retouch specialists, or animators just so you could have a snazzy print headline or a dazzling video title? But now it's *everywhere*. It's everywhere because the software that enables such effects is available and affordable for the designer middle-class (designers who don't have international clients and unlimited budgets)!

The typographic possibilities would have been unthinkable a relatively short time ago: Type that's partially blended into a photograph or embossed with a texture; photomontages rendered on top of headlines; textures and effects that look photographic but were created from scratch on a computer; patterns that have never even been created before; animated, editable fonts for video that explode, burn, wiggle, or do anything you can imagine. If you really want to dazzle 'em, this one's for you.

. . . . . . . . . . . . . . . . . . . . . . . . . . . . . . . . . . . . . . . . . . . . . . . . . . . .

# 4. Most Obvious Trend: Abundance of Font Choices

For many years I felt that I was familiar with every typeface available. Even if some got past me, it was very seldom that I saw a typeface and didn't know its name or at least recognize it. And it was *guaranteed* that I knew every font available in my local area. Plus every style of press type available at the local art supply store. Here's another "that was then" pause. Now I can't even remember all the fonts on my own computer, much less have a comprehensive idea of all the available fonts from the outside world.

I was looking at a friend's type catalog recently and I didn't know a single font in the entire catalog. Everyone's on the font bandwagon. It's not just the large, professional typesetting houses buying fonts out there anymore—it's millions of desktop publishers expressing their individual and eclectic tastes. Traditional type designers are generating new designs, both classical and grungy. New type design companies are springing up and making quite an impact. Freelance designers are designing fonts. Fonts are being designed specifically for web pages and low-resolution monitors. Robin's daughter Scarlett designed a font (named Scarlett) when she was seven years old—and I've seen it used in full color brochures both here in the USA and in Europe.

Fonts used to be very expensive. Now vendors practically give them away. As a matter of fact, sometimes they do give them away. In addition to commercial font prices dropping tremendously, there's a large and growing collection of shareware and freeware fonts available. Don't plan on collecting them all unless you have a hard drive with several terabytes of space.

You may argue that you'll never use or even see half of these fonts. That may be true, but until the government limits type usage to Times and Helvetica, font creation is a huge trend.

# 5. Most Fun Trend: Breaking the Rules

Breaking the rules of design. Big deal. "I do it everyday," you say. That's partly because the rules are fairly subjective and trying to agree on exactly what the rules are could cause a Holy Graphics War. Going out on a graphic limb or out on a design ledge is pretty common, even encouraged. The rules I'm talking about are the untouchable sacred cows of legibility and readability. If there's one rule that I made sure I *never* broke, it was this one: no matter how wild and unorthodox the design, you *had* to be able *at least* to read the copy. Ah, those were the good old days. Fortunately, not many designers are feeling compelled to carry their desktop creations this far. But on the other hand, there are enough people pushing the conventional legibility envelope (even normal, well-adjusted designers) that I'm proclaiming this an official recognizable trend. I know, I know . . . you're probably saying, "I'll believe it's a trend when *Robin Williams* designs a grungy type book." Start believing. Robin wrote that one already—several years ago.*

*\*See A Blip in the continuum by Robin Williams, illustrated by John Tollett*

· · · · · · · · · · · · · · · · · · · · · · · · · · · · · · · · · · · · · · · · · · · · · · · · · ·

# 6. Most Important Trend: Typographic Independence

In the past, our design choices were limited. First, our font choices were limited to whatever our typesetter had decided to include in her library. Her choices were usually the most mainstream, commercially acceptable, and popular font designs. Now, with the large commercial libraries, freeware, and shareware (and all of them available online), our choices are almost unlimited. If you think you're going to run out of choices, you can create your own font design.

Next, we were limited by time and budgets. Okay, those limitations are still there, but they've been minimized by our ability to experiment, create, and produce typographic design on our computers for a fraction of the time and money it used to take. The argument you still hear from the disappearing contingent of desktop critics is that computers just can't deliver the finesse that a type master can give you. I always wondered who those type masters were and why they never worked the midnight shift while my job was being set. My beloved x-acto knife saved a lot of typesetting jobs, but it can't compete anymore. So to the typesetter who once kicked me out of her office because I wanted her to reset some type: Game over, man.

**Typographic Independence is here!**

. . . . . . . . . . . . . . . . . . . . . . . . . . . . . . . . . . . . . . . . . . . . . . . . . . . . . . . . . .

# Future Trends

This is the exciting part. Some of our documents are no longer flat images of type and photographs fixed to a static page. With the advent of the web, many documents are interactive and dynamic. A headline can animate while it moves around on the page; a logo can change into a headline with the click of the mouse; type can change colors or size; and 3D type can rotate or spin. While all this sounded futuristic not long ago, it's commonplace on the web and in video. Certainly a future trend is more interactive type.

Even when designing print material, type can be interactive. OpenType is a "smart" font format—in the right application, you will see characters automatically change their letterforms based on the characters to the left and right. Hyphens and dashes raise and lower themselves depending on whether the text is in caps or not; letterspacing adjusts itself depending on how large or small the type is. Amazing.

Another future trend is the design and use of more fonts created specifically for display on computer monitors. The driving force for font technology up to this point has always been to optimize the output quality for publishing in the print media, but fonts designed for web publishing and video are making a splash and will likely influence print design as well.

As web technology, programming languages, and the speed of Internet access improves, designers will have more freedom in typography, and the creative possibilities of typographic design will be more versatile and more powerful than ever before.

So, in the future, when a student intern in the cubicle down the hall is trying a new holographic feature on a cutting-edge multimedia document, I'll just have one thing to say: "Go get your own x-acto knife, dude. This one's got sentimental value."

# BE NOT

too tame neither,

but let your own discretion be your tutor;

suit the font to the word,

the word to the font...

paraphrased (forgive me) from HAMLET

# Glossary of Type Terms

In which to discern
an apex from an
ascender and an
orphan from a widow.

# Type Terms

## A

**alignment:** Refers to whether text is aligned on the left (flush left), the right (flush right), on both edges (justified), or centered.

**all caps:** When you set type in all capital letters.

**ampersand:** Name of the "&" symbol that stands for the word "and." The symbol is derived from the Latin word "et," which means "and."

**apertures:** Partially open spaces within letters such as C, G, S, a, c. Fully enclosed spaces, as in the letter O, are called *counters.*

**apex:** The top point of a capital letter, such as the peak of a capital A.

**arrangement:** See *alignment.*

**arm:** Horizontal stroke of a letter that is unattached at one end. A capital E has three arms.

**ascender:** The part of a lowercase letter that rises above the height of the lowercase x.

**asterisk:** The * symbol, often called a star.

**asymmetrical:** Not even or equal on both sides.

**ATM:** Adobe Type Manager. A utility that smooths the edges of font characters onscreen. ATM is no longer needed in Mac OS X or Windows XP.

**auto kerning:** When a software program accesses the *kern pairs* built into a typeface.

**axis:** A line through the thinnest parts of a letter O in a typeface that has a *thick/thin* stroke contrast.

*The picture font on these pages is Renfield's Lunch, by Mary-Anne King, available at GarageFonts.com.*

## B

**ball terminal:** The round ball at the end of the arm in letters such as a, c, and r. It's most common in modern typefaces.

**bar:** Horizontal crossbar connecting two sides of a letter, as in A or H.

**baseline:** The invisible line on which type sits (excluding *descenders*).

**beak:** The *serif* at the end of an *arm*, such as in E and L.

**bitmapped font:** The part of a font that is created with and displayed on the screen with pixels, as opposed to *outlines.*

**blackletter:** A style of type, also called German Blackletter, Gothic and mistakenly Old English. 𝕿𝖍𝖎𝖘 𝖎𝖘 𝖇𝖑𝖆𝖈𝖐𝖑𝖊𝖙𝖙𝖊𝖗.

**bleed:** Any element on a page that is printed over the trimmed edge of the paper.

**body:** Sometimes the *x-height* is called the body of a typeface.

**body clearance:** Horizontal space designed into the typeface above the ascenders and below the descenders so the lines of type don't touch each other.

**body copy:** Text type set in paragraphs. Point sizes range from about 8 to 12 point.

**bold face:** A font variation that has thicker strokes in the letterforms.

**bounding box:** The invisible rectangle that surrounds blocks of text or graphics in software programs.

**bowl:** The curved stroke that makes an enclosed space within a letter, such as the stroke that encloses the *counter* on the letter b.

**bracket:** The curve that connects some serifs and the stems of letters.

**bracketed serif:** Serif that is connected to the main stroke of a letter by a small curved stroke (the *bracket*).

**bullet:** A dot (•), box (■), or other tiny element used as a graphic in text, often to indicate an item in a list.

· · · · · · · · · · · · · · · · · · · · · · · · · · · · · · · · · · · · · · · · · · · · · · ·

# C

**cap height:** The height of the capital letters within a typeface. The cap height may be greater than or less than ascender height.

**capitals:** The uppercase letters of the alphabet, affectionately called "caps."

**caption:** Text accompanying a photo or illustration.

**center alignment/centered:** The text on each line is centered within the line length.

**character:** One single letter, number, punctuation mark, etc.

**character set:** The entire set of all the letters, numbers, symbols, punctuation, dingbats, etc., within a font.

**characters per pica (cpp):** A measurement of how many characters in a particular face and size could fit in a pica. Before *desktop publishing*, knowing the cpp of a font was necessary for calculating the fit of type.

**cicero:** A unit of measure slightly larger than the pica. One cicero equals 0.178 inch, 12 didot points, or 12.75 PostScript points.

**Clarendon:** The name of a type family in the slab serif category. Sometimes the entire category is called Clarendon because the face is a perfect example of a slab serif.

**color:** The overall tone, density, and texture of a page of type in black and white.

**column:** Type set in vertical sections separated by a blank space (gutter). This glossary is set in two columns of type per page.

**condensed type:** Type that has a narrower character width than regular text type, useful for fitting a lot of copy in a small space.

**contrast:** The difference between the thin and thick strokes of a letterform. Or the overall difference between the looks of different typefaces.

**copy:** All the text on a page or in a document.

**copyfitting:** Calculating how much space is needed to fit a certain amount of type.

**counter:** Fully or partially enclosed white space within a letter.

**crop marks:** Thin lines at each of the four corners of a page that define the outer edges of the document.

**curly quotes:** A descriptive name for true *quotation marks*.

**cursive:** Type that flows, such as script or italic fonts.

# D

**decorative face:** A typeface designed for a distinctive, ornate, or otherwise graphic look.

**descender:** The part of a letter that extends below the *baseline*.

**desktop publishing (dtp):** The use of the personal computer to create (publish) pages that contain text and graphics.

**didot:** A unit of measure similar to a *point*. Twelve didot points make one *cicero*, similar to a *pica*.

**dingbats:** Decorative elements such as symbols, icons, or ornaments. These may be entire fonts or individual *glyphs* contained within a font. Zapf Dingbats and Wingdings are well-known examples.

**discretionary hyphen (dischy):** A hyphen you can type in your software that disappears when it's not needed.

**display type:** Type over the size of 14 point, as in headlines or advertising titles.

**dotless i:** A lowercase i with no dot. This is useful when the dot bumps into another letter or when you want an accent over the letter instead of the dot. To type a dotless i on a Mac, press Shift Option B.

**dpi:** Dots per inch, a measure of the *resolution* of a printer and of the text and images on a printed page. Also see *ppi.*

**drop cap:** A large or ornate letter at the beginning of a paragraph, also called an initial cap.

**drop out type:** When you put text on top of an image and "drop out" the text so the white of the paper shows through where the type is.

**dumb quotes:** Fake quotation marks like those made on the typewriter ("). A painfully obvious sign of unprofessional type.

· · · · · · · · · · · · · · · · · · · · · · · · · · · · · · · · · · · · · · ·

# E

**ear:** Small stroke projecting from the top of the lowercase g.

**Egyptian:** A category of type that has slab serifs and little contrast in the strokes. The category is also known as slab serifs.

**elite:** A monospaced typewriter typeface that sets 12 characters per inch.

**ellipsis:** Three dots (…) used to indicate an omission of text or a thought that trails off.

**em:** A horizontal unit of measure equal to the point size of the type in use. It's about the width of the capital letter M.

**em dash:** A long dash used to indicate a shift in thought—it sets off emphatic material that is too important to put in parentheses.

**em space:** A non-breaking space as wide as the point size of the type in use.

**en:** A horizontal unit of measure equal to half the point size of the type in use. It's about the width of the capital letter N.

**en dash:** A dash used to indicate a range, as in 9–5. Use as a substitute for the word "to."

**en space:** A non-breaking space half as wide as the point size of the type in use.

**expert set:** Additions to basic font sets that contain alternate and special characters such as *small caps, swash characters,* and *oldstyle numerals.*

**extended type:** Type that has a wider character width than regular text type.

**extenders:** *Ascenders* and *descenders.*

**eye:** The *counter* (enclosed space) of the lowercase "e."

# F

**family:** A font family contains all the related fonts with the same design characteristics and the same name.

**figure space:** A space that is the same width as a *lining figure* (number).

**finial:** The tapered, curved end of a stroke not ending in a serif (c, e). Also a variation of a letter for use as the last letter in a line.

**first-line indent:** The indent of the first line after you hit Return or Enter.

**fleuron:** A typographical ornament, often leaf or flower shaped.

**flush left:** Text *aligned* on the left.

**flush right:** Text *aligned* on the right.

**folio:** A page number.

**font:** One weight, width, and style of a typeface.

**font family:** See *family.*

**font ID conflict:** Some operating systems and programs identify a font by its number, some by its name. It is possible to have fonts installed with the same number or the same name and this can cause conflicts.

**font ID number:** Every font on the Mac is identified by a particular number.

**font management:** Using a program that allows you to open and close fonts as needed, create font sets, and handle font ID conflicts and corrupt fonts.

**font metrics:** The detailed design specifications of the font, such as the thickness of the underline, how tall the capital letters are, the kerning pairs, etc.

**footer:** The repeating text that appears at the bottoms of document pages. Also known as the "running foot." It might include a page number, date, etc.

**format:** To apply certain characteristics (font, size, style) to the words on the page.

**fraction bar:** A non-breaking slash used in fractions. It's slightly different from a regular slash in that it's a bit thinner and tilts more.

**fringe type:** Distorted or deliberately trashed type, often difficult to read, but fun to use.

# G

**glyph:** A symbol that represents a character. For instance, in an OpenType font you might have eight different glyphs that all represent the letter A.

**gothic:** A name sometimes used for sans serif or blackletter fonts.

**gutter:** The vertical blank space that separates columns or pages.

**hairline:** Thinnest stroke in a character, specifically in the modern category.

**hairline rule:** One-quarter point *stroke* or line.

**hairline serif:** A flat, thin serif as on a letter in a modern typeface.

**hanging indent:** When the first line of a paragraph hangs out to the left of the rest of the paragraph. Also known as an *outdent.*

**hanging punctuation:** Punctuation that is moved beyond the edge of the text to avoid the appearance of an indent.

**hard copy:** A printed copy. "Hard" means you can touch it.

**hard line break:** When you press Shift Return or Shift Enter to force a line to break, but it does not create a new paragraph.

**hard Return:** When you press the Return/ Enter key to manually start a new paragraph.

**hard space:** A non-breaking space between two words. A hard space prevents those words from being separated at the ends of lines.

**header:** Text that is repeated at the top of each document page. Also called a *running head.*

**headline:** The title of a body of text.

**hints:** Extra information included in some fonts that ensures optimal appearance and output.

**hyphenation zone:** A designated width at the right margin whose measurement determines if words will hyphenate or not.

**I-beam:** The text cursor that you use to select text or move the *insertion point.*

**icon:** A little picture that represents a file on your computer.

**imagesetter:** A large, high-end PostScript printer used for high-resolution output on paper or film.

**indent:** The amount of space between the *margins* of a page and the actual text.

**inferior:** See *subscript.*

**initial cap:** See *drop cap.*

**insertion point:** When you click the *I-beam* in text, it sets a flashing bar known as the insertion point. The insertion point indicates where text will appear when you start to type and where a graphic will appear when you insert it.

**italic:** A style of type where the letters slant to the right. True-drawn italics do not simply slant—they have been completely redesigned.

**jump line:** A brief line at the end of a column or page telling the reader where the text continues.

**justified:** Text that is aligned on both the left and right sides of the text block.

**kern, kerning:** The process of adjusting the space between letters so the spacing appears to be visually consistent.

**kern pairs:** Pairs of letters that have tighter spacing built into them so they tuck into each other nicely.

**leaders:** A series of repeated periods, dots, or other little symbols that lead your eye from one column to the next, as in a table of contents.

**leading:** (pronounced "ledding") The amount of space between the *baseline* of one line of text and the next baseline.

**legibility:** How easy it is to tell one letter from another in any given typeface, which determines how easy it is to read short bursts of type like headlines or signage.

· · · · · · · · · · · · · · · · · · · · · · · · · · · · · · · · · · · · · · · · · · · · · · · · · · · ·

**letterspacing:** The space from one character to the next.

Also, if you "letterspace" a line or block of text, it implies that you added extra space, sometimes lots of space, between all the characters to create a certain graphic effect.

**ligature:** A special character combining two or more characters into one.

**line break:** The point at which any line ends. This is different from a *hard line break.*

**line spacing:** See *leading.*

**lining figures/numbers:** Numerals that are the same height as the capital letters in a typeface. "Tabular lining figures" will align in columns.

**link:** The stroke connecting the top and bottom parts of a letter, as in the lowercase g.

**loop:** The lower portion of a lowercase g.

**lowercase:** The small letters of an alphabet.

**margin:** The white space between the copy on the page and the trimmed edge of the paper.

**mark-up:** To take a pen and write typesetting specifications all over the page.

**measure:** The width of a column or the length of a line of type.

**metrics:** See *font metrics.*

**modern type:** A category of type that has a strong thick-thin contrast in the stroke weights and thin horizontal serifs.

**monospaced:** A font whose characters each take up the same amount of space. That is, a period uses the same width space as a capital W.

**monoweight:** The strokes of a letterform have very little difference in thickness all the way around.

**negative leading:** A *leading* measurement in which the leading value is smaller than the *point size* of the type. For example, 24/20 would be negative leading.

**nonbreaking characters:** Special characters (such as hyphens or slashes) that force words or fractions to stay together even at the ends of lines.

**nonbreaking space:** A word space that keeps two words together, preventing them from breaking onto two separate lines.

**oblique:** Slanted type, typical of most sans serif "italic" faces (but not all).

**offset printing:** A process of printing in which the image goes from a special printing plate, onto an intermediary roller and then is printed onto the paper.

**oldstyle figures/numbers:** Numerals with ascender and descenders that blend well with lowercase letters. They might be *proportional* or *lining.*

**oldstyle type:** A category of serif type with moderate *stroke* contrast and diagonal *stress.* Easy on the eyes and easy to read.

**OpenType:** A cross-platform file format that can contain over 65,000 characters. Not all operating systems or software programs can handle OpenType fonts.

**optical kerning:** Automatic kerning based on the shapes of the letters.

**optical size:** A font optimized for specific point sizes. For instance, you might have a display font specifically for type larger than 14 to 18 point, or a caption font specifically for small type sizes.

**orphan:** The last line of a paragraph alone at the top of a column or page, or the first line of a paragraph alone at the bottom of a column or page.

**outdent:** The first line or first several lines of a paragraph start to the left of the rest of the text. Also called a *hanging indent.*

**outline font:** A font in which each character is stored as a mathematical "outline" of the character shape. Also known as a *scalable font* and a *printer font.*

**output:** Whatever comes out of your computer, such as hard copy from the printer.

P

**pagination:** The process of putting pages into consecutive order.

**pair kerning:** Using the pairs of kerned characters that a designer has built into a font. See also *pair kerns.*

**pi font:** A typeface with mathematical and scientific characters.

**pica:** A typographic measurement of twelve *points.* Six picas equal one inch.

**pica:** On a typewriter, a pica is a generic, *monospaced* font that has ten characters per inch (as opposed to *elite,* which has twelve).

**picture font:** A font that has little pictures instead of characters. Useful for logos, bullets, decorative borders. The small images on these glossary pages are all picture fonts.

**point:** The smallest typographic measurement. In digital typography, there are 72 points per inch, 12 points per pica. Traditionally (in hot metal), there were 72.27 points per inch.

**point size:** The measurement of type at a particular size. You are reading 9-point type. Also see *point.*

**PostScript:** A programming language designed specifically for printing electronic documents.

**PostScript font:** A font designed for use with the PostScript printing process.

**ppi:** Pixels per inch, a measure of the digital resolution of an image on the screen.

**prime marks:** Symbols used to indicate inches and feet and hours and minutes.

**printer font:** The component of a *PostScript* font that enables the font to print to a PostScript printer. Also called an *outline font.*

**proof:** Final printed draft. If the proof is perfect, then you can proceed to printing your final version, ready for reproduction

**proportional spacing:** The characters each take up a relative, or proportional, amount of space according to how wide they are. That is, a cap W takes up more space than a lowercase i.

**pull quote:** A passage of text emphasized on the page in a graphic way.

**punctuation:** All the characters in a font that are used to define our grammar, such as commas, questions marks, periods, etc.

Q

**queue:** An orderly line, such as jobs waiting to print.

**quotation marks:** Punctuation marks used to mark the beginning and end of quoted material.

**range kerning:** Adjusting the letterspacing over a range (group) of characters.

**readability:** How easy it is to read a large amount of text.

**recto:** The right-hand page in a book, always odd-numbered.

**resolution:** How clearly "resolved" an image or typeface looks on the screen (measured in *ppi*) or when printed (measured in *dpi*).

**reverse:** The opposite of the standard of black text on a white background—white text on a black (or dark) background. As opposed to *drop out.*

**river:** Poor wordspacing in justified copy creates a "river" of white space that flows vertically through the text.

**roman:** Any typeface, serif or sans serif, that does not slant. This font is roman.

**rule:** Typesetter jargon for a drawn line. A rule's thickness is measured in points, as in a "3-point rule."

**run-around:** When text flows around the edges of a graphic or shape. Also known as a *text wrap.*

**running head:** Repetitive text that appears at the tops of document pages.

. . . . . . . . . . . . . . . . . . . . . . . . . . . . . . . . . . . . . . . . . . . . . . . . . .

## S

**sans serif:** A category of type that does not have *serifs*. The bold type in these definitions is a sans serif font.

**scalable font:** A font that can be resized to any point size without becoming distorted, either on the screen or the printed page.

**screen font:** The bitmapped part of some fonts used to display the type on the screen. Also known as a *bitmapped font*. It is one component of a PostScript Type 1 font.

**script:** Typefaces that emulate handwriting.

**serif:** A very short line that extends from upper and lower ends of main strokes. There are many variations—cupped, rounded, square, slab, bracketed etc.

**service bureau:** A business that produces high-resolution output of digital files. They use an *imagesetter* and print to a variety of color devices or to film.

**set solid:** A leading measurement in which the *leading* value is the same as the *point size* of the type, such as 20/20.

**set width:** The horizontal width that is built into a character when it is designed.

**shoulder:** Curved stroke of a letter with a convex shape, as in h, m, and n.

**slab serif type:** A category of type that is *monoweight* with thick, flat serifs. Also known as *Egyptian* type.

**small caps:** Capital letters that are approximately the size of lowercase letters.

**smart apostrophe:** Refers to a true apostrophe, not a straight one. ' not '.

**smart quote:** Refers to true quote marks, not straight ones, such as " and ", not " and ".

**soft Return:** A soft Return is sometimes mistakenly thought of as a *hard line break,* where you press Shift Return/Enter to force a new line without starting a new paragraph. But a soft Return is really when the text bumps into the right indent and automatically returns to the left indent. This is sometimes also known as "word wrap."

**solid:** See *set solid.*

**spine:** Central curved stroke of the letter S.

**spur:** Small projection off a main stroke, found on many capital Gs.

**standoff:** In a *text wrap*, the distance between text and the graphic around which the text is wrapping.

**stem:** Main vertical or diagonal stroke of a letter.

**stress:** Direction of thickening on the curved stroke of a letter.

**stroke:** Any straight or curved line of a character.

**style sheet:** A collection of formatting options that can be applied easily and consistently to text. Style sheets are the most important and time-saving feature in page layout and word processing software.

**subscript:** A small character written beneath another one, such as the lower number in a fraction or the 2 in $H_2O$.

**superior/superscript:** A small character written above and/or to the side of another character. The top half of a fraction or the letters following an ordinal number (1st, 3d, 5th) are common examples.

**swash characters:** Specially designed letter-forms that have *tails* or elaborate shapes, such as *Q* or *R.*

## T

**tabular figures:** Numerals designed to be *monospaced* so they will line up in columns of numbers.

**tail:** The descender of Q or the diagonal stroke at the bottom of R or j.

**terminal:** The end of a stroke of a letter that doesn't end with a serif, as in e or r.

**text wrap:** When the edge of a text block wraps around the edge of a graphic.

**thick/thin:** Refers to the change of stroke weight in a letterform as it moves from the thin point to the thicker part.

**thin space:** A non-breaking space one-quarter width of the point size in use.

**tracking:** Adjusting the space between *glyphs* in a range of text. Often this is called range *kerning.*

**true-drawn:** Refers to typeface variations that have been drawn by the type designer rather than modified by the computer.

**TrueType:** An *outline* font developed by Apple and Microsoft.

**type family:** A group of fonts that includes all the members of a single typeface *family*.

**Type 1 font:** A high-quality *PostScript outline* font.

**typeface:** A collection of letters, numbers, symbols, etc that share a specific design.

**type size:** The size of the type measured in *points*.

**type style:** A variation within a type family, such as a weight or width variations. For instance, italic is a type style.

**typo:** Short for "typographical error."

**typographic color:** See *color*. Letter- and word-spacing, leading, ink, and paper colors affect the "color" of the type, even if the type is all black.

**typography:** The art or process of designing with type and letterforms.

**unbracketed serif:** A serif without a small curved stroke (a *bracket*) connecting it to the stem of the letter.

**underline:** A line directly under the type, put there by using a menu command or keyboard shortcut (as opposed to a *rule*). Never use an underline in professional-level type.

**Unicode:** A coding system that creates fonts that can contain more than 65,000 glyphs, as opposed to the ASCII format that can only contain 256 glyphs. Not all operating systems and software applications use Unicode.

**uppercase:** Capital letters of the alphabet.

**U/lc, upper and lowercase:** Capital and lowercase letters used together, as opposed to *all caps*.

**verso:** The left-hand page of a book or newsletter, always even-numbered.

**weight:** The thickness of the strokes that form the characters in the font.

**white space:** The space in and around the type and graphic elements on a page.

**widow:** A very short (proportionally) last line of a paragraph.

**width:** One of the variations possible in a type family describing the horizontal width of characters. Ranges from ultra-condensed to ultra-expanded.

**word spacing:** The space between words created by pressing the Spacebar.

**WYSIWYG:** What You See Is What You Get. This refers to whether the text and images you *see* on your screen match what you actually *get* when it's printed.

**x-height:** Height of the body of lowercase letters, excluding ascenders and descenders.

# Your attitude is your life.

Robin Williams *(not the actor)*

# Other Info

In which there is
important information
regarding the
fonts in this book,
setting special
characters,
and several font
utilities.

# Appendix A
## Listen to your eyes

### Kerning, Tracking, and Letterspacing in InDesign:
### Why It's Important and When to Use It

Excellent letterspacing isn't the sexiest thing InDesign can do, but it makes the difference between good type and great type, and it displays the difference between a good designer and a great designer. Inappropriate or unconscious letterspacing can make type difficult to read, difficult to comprehend, and difficult to respect.

There is no formulaic method for adjusting the spaces between letters—it is entirely dependent on the typeface, the type size, the paper, the color of ink, the purpose of the piece. The final judge is your eyes. Your eyes know if the spacing is uneven, too tight, or too loose. Listen to your eyes. Listen to your eyes and know how to control your software.

# Watermelon
# Watermelon

InDesign has controls for kerning, tracking, letterspacing, and word spacing, and all of these individual controls are affected by the justification, hyphenation, and composition settings. So we'll start at the most intimate level and move up to the most global. But first let's look at the preference that controls your kerning values. You should change this preference when you have no document open on your screen—this will set the value as the default for all *new* documents.

· · · · · · · · · · · · · · · · · · · · · · · · · · · · · · · · · · · · · · · · · · · ·

From the InDesign menu, choose "Preferences…," then "Units & Increments…." You see that the default kerning value is "20" thousandths of an em. This means if you take the point size of the type (which is called an em), say 24 point, and divide it into 1000 parts, each default kerning space is 20/1000, which is much too much. Change this to 5 units and click OK.

*Change the kerning value to 5.*

### Auto kern pairs, the lowest common denominator

Now, a well-designed typeface includes a number of auto kern pairs. Certain pairs of letters always need kerning, such as "To" or "Va." A well-designed face has the kerning built into the font metrics so when you type certain combinations of characters, they tuck into each other nicely. A font might have anywhere from fifty to several thousand auto kern pairs. InDesign, by default, applies these auto kern pairs, as you can tell by the kerning field: it typically says "Metrics."

This means it's using the font metrics and applying the kerning value built into the font. That's why when you click the insertion point between two characters, this same kerning field displays a number in parentheses—that's the kerning value of the auto pair. (That's also why type automatically looks better in InDesign than it does in most word processors because most word processors don't apply the auto kern pairs.)

. . . . . . . . . . . . . . . . . . . . . . . . . . . . . . . . . . . . . . . . . . . . . . . . . .

If you use a typeface that does not have built-in kern pairs, or if you use a combination of fonts, styles, or sizes, that's when you want to use the "Optical" option in the kerning field. Optical looks at the shapes of the letters and tries to adjust them as well as it can—without eyes.

*This is a typeface designed by my daughter when she was seven years old; it has very few kerning pairs so I turned on the Optical kerning.*

## Manual kerning

Manual kerning means to adjust the space between two characters, and it's the most important letterspacing feature because it is the only one dependent on your eyes. This is what you'll use to fine-tune your text after all the other options have been adjusted.

When you use the keyboard shortcut to kern, InDesign applies the amount you have set in the preferences pane you changed earlier. That is, if you put the insertion point between two characters and use the keyboard shortcut Option LeftArrow, each tap of the left arrow removes 5/1000 of an em. Option RightArrow increases the space 5/1000 of an em.

Hold down the Command key in addition to the Option and arrow keys and you decrease or increase the amount by five. That is, Command Option LeftArrow removes 25/1000 of an em instead of 5.

Any manual kerning you apply is added to the auto pair kern that might be built into the two characters. The kerning field displays the total amount of the auto pair kern and any manual kerning you apply.

Note: The kerning value is applied to the character *on the left.* You can copy and paste that character and the kerning value goes with it. Delete the character and the kerning is deleted.

. . . . . . . . . . . . . . . . . . . . . . . . . . . . . . . . . . . . . . . . . . . . . . . . .

### Tracking

Tracking means to adjust the space between a selected range of characters. Instead of applying an individual amount between a pair of letters, tracking applies the same amount to all the characters that are selected. Because tracking does not take into account the shapes of the letters, it's really only useful to get a start on adjusting the space—you'll still need to fine tune with manual kerning.

Any tracking you apply is added to the manual kerning and to the auto pair kerns. That's why you might select an entire word and apply one value of tracking, but when you click between two characters in that same word, the kerning field displays a different value. But the tracking value does not affect the kerning value! You can manually kern between individual characters until they are visually consistent, then apply tracking and everything will tighten or loosen proportionally.

Use the same keyboard shortcuts for tracking as for kerning. To track, select a range of text first.

> **Tips:** To remove all kerning and tracking (but not the auto pair kerns), select the text and hit Command Option Q.
>
> To remove the auto kern pairs, select the text and choose "0" in the kerning field menu.

### Paragraph-specific letterspacing

The kerning and tracking values are "character-specific," meaning you can apply them to selected characters. But sometimes you want to open up the letterspacing in an entire paragraph of text, a story, or an entire document.

Because letterspacing does not take into consideration any tracking or kerning or pair kern values, it is the fastest and most processor-efficient way for InDesign to adjust the space between lots of characters. This is the feature you want to use if you have a lot of text to open up or tighten. You won't see the paragraph letterspacing value reflected in the tracking or kerning fields.

To adjust the paragraph letterspacing, use the "Justification" dialog box in either your style sheet options or from the "Paragraph" palette menu; see the following page.

• • • • • • • • • • • • • • • • • • • • • • • • • • • • • • • • • • • • • • • • • •

We're only going to use the first two rows of specs in this dialog box. Now, there are two things to remember about these specs:

One, the "Minimum" and "Maximum" amounts only apply if you justify the text. That is, text that is set flush right or flush left will ignore whatever is in those fields.

Two, the "Desired" amount must be between the "Minimum" and "Maximum." So if you want to change the "Desired" letterspacing to 25 percent, first you must change the "Maximum" to 25 percent or more.

Just as with kern pairs, the typeface designer has built into the font the amount of space on the sides of each character, particularly the right side, or the "pen advance." The percentages that you enter in the "Justification" dialog box are how much you want to *deviate* from the amount that is built into the font metrics.

You probably know that the smaller the type size, the more letterspacing it needs, proportionally, and the larger the type, the less letterspacing it needs. So let's say you have a large block of small type and you want to open up the space a little. You could do it with tracking, but it will be faster and more efficient to use the paragraph letterspacing.

So select the text. In the "Justification" dialog box, first enter an amount in the Letter Spacing "Maximum" field. If your text is justified, enter the percentage that you want to increase the spacing by, and enter that same amount in the "Desired" field. If your text is not justified, enter any amount in the "Maximum" field, then enter your desired increase in the "Desired" field.

If you're working with large type that needs less letterspacing, you can enter negative numbers in the "Minimum" and "Desired" fields.

. . . . . . . . . . . . . . . . . . . . . . . . . . . . . . . . . . . . . . . . . . . . . . . . . . . .

### Paragraph-specific wordspacing

The Word Spacing in the "Justification" dialog box works the same as Letter Spacing: The designer has built into the font metrics the "spaceband," or the amount of space that appears on the page when you hit the Spacebar. You can *deviate* from this amount by a desired percentage. In a number of fonts I open up the word spacing just a wee bit for clarity.

There's a great keyboard shortcut for manually kerning just the spacebands (the word spacing) in selected text; see the chart on the following page.

### But wait—there's more!

Now, after all the work you put into adjusting the letterspacing, tracking, and kerning of your type, your carefully chosen specs are further influenced by the hyphenation controls you set and the composing method you choose. And InDesign can't always do what you want, especially if you justify the text. But that's another story.

For now, become familiar with the manual kerning, manual tracking, and automatic letterspacing features. Know when and why to use each one and how to have complete control over them. **And listen to your eyes.**

· · · · · · · · · · · · · · · · · · · · · · · · · · · · · · · · · · · · · · · · · · · · · ·

## Letterspacing chart for InDesign

**KERNING** applies when the insertion point is flashing between two characters. The kerning value is actually applied to the glyph on the left.

> **Auto pair-kerns** and **Metrical kerning:** Default
>
> **Optical kerning:** Use when a font has minimal pair kerns or when mixing typefaces.
>
> Click between two characters after applying Optical kerning to see the exact value in parentheses.
>
> **Manual kerning:** Insertion point is between two characters.
>
> | | | |
> |---|---|---|
> | **Add space:** | *Option RightArrow* | *Alt RightArrow* |
> | **Delete space:** | *Option LeftArrow* | *Alt LeftArrow* |
> | **x5 increment:** | *Add the Command key (Mac) or Control key (PC) to the above* | |

**TRACKING** applies when more than one character is selected.

> **Tracking:** Adds to the manual kerning (if any) and auto pair-kerns.
>
> *Same shortcuts as above*

**REMOVE** all kerning and tracking from selected text.

> | | | |
> |---|---|---|
> | **Remove:** | *Command Option Q* | *Control Alt Q* |

**PARAGRAPH-SPECIFIC** letterspacing

> This applies the same value between all letters in the entire paragraph; does *not* take into account the auto pair-kerns as tracking does.
>
> Use the "Justification" dialog box. *(Command Option Shift J)*
>
> "Minimum" and "Maximum" only affect text when justified.
>
> "Desired" must be between Minimum and Maximum.

**WORD SPACING**

> **Manual word kerning**
>
> | | | |
> |---|---|---|
> | **Add space:** | *Command Option \* | *Control Alt \* |
> | **Delete space:** | *Command Option Delete* | *Control Alt Backspace* |
> | **x5 increment:** | add the Shift key to above | |
>
> **Paragraph-specific word spacing:** Use the "Justification" dialog box, as explained above.

**VISUALLY DISPLAY** custom kerning or tracking

> Use the Composition preferences; check "Custom Tracking/Kerning."

# Appendix B
# Font & Product Vendors

## Font Vendors

**Altemus Collection**
An artistic collection
of dingbat fonts.
www.Altemus.com

**Luc Devroye**
Links to fonts in different
languages, history, articles.
http://jeff.cs.mcgill.ca/~luc/
fonts.html

**Atomic Media**
Bitmap fonts that are
perfect for Flash, web,
and WAP design.
www.AtomicMedia.net

**Font Bureau**
Custom typefaces
and retail fonts.
www.FontBureau.com

**FontFreak**
Thousands of free and
shareware fonts, plus links
to font software.
www.FontFreak.com

**FontGeek**
A valuable collection of
advice, information, fixes, and
news about using fonts in
Mac OS X and professional
graphic design applications.
www.FontGeek.net

**FontHaus Inc.**
Fonts, clip art, illustrations,
and stock photos.
www.FontHaus.com

**FontShop**
Over 30,000 fonts
by many designers.
www.FontShop.com

**The FontSite**
Fonts, articles, and more.
www.FontSite.com

**GarageFonts**
Over 750 typefaces from
designers around the globe.
www.GarageFonts.com

**Hoefler & Frere-Jones**
A library of original and
licensed fonts.
www.Typography.com

**International Typeface
Corporation (ITC)**
Over 1500 fonts and an
informative web site.
www.ITCfonts.com

**LetterPerfect**
Original display fonts
and custom lettering.
www.Letterspace.com

**Linotype**
More than 6,000 fonts, plus
lots of articles and info.
www.Linotype.com

**Monotype Corporation**
Not only fonts, but articles,
news, technology, and more.
Monotype is forming a non-
profit organization dedicated
to the advancement of the
typographic arts.
www.Fonts.com

**My Fonts**
Find, try, and buy fonts.
They will also help you
identify fonts.
www.MyFonts.com

**P22**
Fonts inspired by art
and history.
www.p22.com

**Phil's Fonts**
More than 35,000 fonts
from 75 foundries.
www.PhilsFonts.com

**Plazm Media Cooperative**
Experimental type foundry
specializing in custom fonts.
www.Plazm.com

**T26**
Fonts, EPS illustrations,
merchandise.
www.T26.com

**Three Islands Press**
Links to OldFonts.com,
TypeQuarry.com, and others.
Specializes in exquisite, old
letterwriting scripts.
www.ThreeIslandsPress.com

**Veer**
Fonts and more! See
what your headline looks
like in any font.
www.Veer.com

## Font Products

**You Control: Fonts
(Mac only)**
Organize your font menu, display fonts in their styles in the menu, choose fonts with a keyboard hotkey, and much much more. $19.95; download a free trial.
www.YouSoftware.com/fonts

**PopChar Pro, PopChar X, PopChar Win**
PopChar X is a utility for easy access to all the characters within a font.
www.Macility.com

**FontLab**
A great resource for all sorts of type tools including Fontographer, a program for font manipulation and creation.
www.FontLab.com

## Font Management Utilities

| | |
|---|---|
| **Extensis Suitcase** | **$99.95** |
| **Font Reserve** | **$99.95** |
| www.Extensis.com | |

**FontAgent Pro $99.95
(Mac only)**
www.InsiderSoftware.com

## Page Layout Applications

**Adobe InDesign
Adobe PageMaker**
www.Adobe.com

**Adobe Studio**
Adobe software tips and tutorials.
www.Adobe.com/studio

**QuarkXPress**
www.Quark.com

## Type Sites

**Chris MacGregor's Internet Type Foundry Index**
This is an incredibly useful site for typophiles. Chris keeps up on who is doing what in the type world and works very hard to maintain this site so it benefits you. He provides a link to every type vendor in the world, plus information on many other aspects of type and a variety of resources. Tell Chris I said hello.
www.TypeIndex.com

**Will-Harris House**
Daniel Will-Harris provides another labor of love, the Will-Harris House, directed to people who care about type. You'll find articles, opinions, humor, and history here. You'll also find an interactive method for determining the most appropriate typeface for a job. Daniel is an expert on working with and using fonts on PCs. Tell Daniel and Toni I said hello.
www.Will-Harris.com

**Typophile**
A member-supported type community with forums, blogs, articles, downloads, merchandise, and more.
www.Typophile.com

**Counterspace**
Type info presented in an interactive format. Get out your reading glasses, however.
Counterspace.Motivo.com

**About.com**
Judy Litt runs a great site on About.com for graphic design and typography. Unfortunately, About.com has added so much advertising and other junk that every site on About has become very difficult to use.
GraphicDesign.About.com

**TypePhases Design**
Illustration fonts, text fonts, and more, plus articles on typography. Includes a great tutorial for managing fonts in Windows, including a number of utilities.
http://inicia.es/de/jmas/

# Appendix C
# Special Characters

This section contains information about the special characters available in most typefaces. If you're using an OpenType font that includes thousands of glyphs in a program that can take advantage of them (like Adobe InDesign), use the Glyphs palette as explained in Chapter 8.

## ANSI chart ▪ Windows

The following characters can usually be added into most word processing and page layout documents by using the ANSI code. To type these codes, hold down the Alt key and type the four numbers (always a zero first) **on the numeric keypad,** then let go of the Alt key. Do not use the numbers across the top of your keyboard! You must use the numeric keypad on the right side of your keyboard.

If you use InDesign, PageMaker, Word, or QuarkXPress on a PC, check your manual—there are regular keyboard shortcuts you can use to insert these characters instead of using the ANSI code. Also check the Character Map, as described on the previous page.

| Character | Type this code | What is it? |
|:---:|:---:|:---|
| ' | Alt 0145 | opening single quote |
| ' | Alt 0146 | closing single quote |
| " | Alt 0147 | opening double quote |
| " | Alt 0148 | closing double quote |
| • | Alt 0149 | bullet |
| – | Alt 0150 | en dash |
| — | Alt 0151 | em dash |
| … | Alt 0133 | ellipsis |
| ™ | Alt 0153 | trademark symbol |
| © | Alt 0169 | copyright symbol |
| ® | Alt 0174 | registration mark |
| ¢ | Alt 0162 | cents symbol |
| £ | Alt 0163 | British pound sterling |
| ¥ | Alt 0165 | Japanese yen |
| é | Alt 0233 | e with acute accent |
| ñ | Alt 0241 | n with tilde |
| € | Alt 0128 | euro symbol in fonts that include it |

· · · · · · · · · · · · · · · · · · · · · · · · · · · · · · · · · · · · · · · · · · ·

| | | |
|---|---|---|
| ¿ | Option Shift ? | inverted question mark |
| ¡ | Option ! | inverted exclamation point |
| ß | Option s | Beta, or German double s (ss) |
| ø | Option o | lowercase letter o with slash |
| Ø | Option Shift O | uppercase letter O with slash |
| ≠ | Option = | does-not-equal sign |
| ≈ | Option x | approximately-equals sign |
| ≤ | Option < *(above the comma)* | less-than-or-equal-to sign |
| ≥ | Option > *(above the period)* | greater-than-or-equal-to sign |
| ± | Option Shift + | plus-or-minus sign |
| ÷ | Option / | division sign |
| √ | Option v | radical sign; square root symbol |
| ƒ | Option f | function symbol or freeze |
| ∫ | Option b | integral symbol |
| ∞ | Option 5 | infinity symbol |
| ¬ | Option l *(the letter el)* | logical NOT, negation symbol |
| ‰ | Option Shift R | salinity symbol |
| ı | Option Shift B | dotless i |
| ª | Option 9 | feminine ordinal indicator |
| º | Option 0 *(zero)* | masculine ordinal indicator |
| ∂ | Option d | lowercase delta |
| Δ | Option j | uppercase delta |
| π | Option p | lowercase pi |
| Π | Option Shift P | uppercase pi |
| μ | Option m | lowercase mu |
| Σ | Option w | uppercase sigma; summation |
| Ω | Option z | uppercase omega |
| ˆ | Option Shift i | circumflex |
| ˘ | Option Shift . *(period)* | breve* |
| ¯ | Option Shift , *(comma)* | macron* |
| · | Option h | dot* |
| ° | Option k | ring* |

*In regular fonts, these diacritical marks cannot be placed above letters, as can the ones below. But if you have an OpenType font, you'll find individual glyphs for all characters that use these marks.*

### Accent marks directly over the letters

| | | | |
|---|---|---|---|
| ~ | Option n | as in ñ in piñata | tilde |
| ´ | Option e | as in é in résumé | acute |
| ` | Option ` *(to left of number 1)* | as in à in voilà | grave |
| ¨ | Option u | as in ï in naïve | diaeresis |
| ˆ | Option i | | circumflex |

To type the letter with the accent mark above it, do this:

Hold down the Option key and type the key noted in this chart (such as Option n). Nothing will appear to happen!

Let go of the Option key, then type the character you want (n).

The character will appear with the accent mark directly over it.

# Index

• • • • • • • • • • • • • • • • • • • • • • • • • • • • • • • • • •

• • • • • • • • • • • • • • • • • • • • • • • • • • • • • • • • • • • • • • • • • • • • • • • • •

## About the Author

I live and work in Santa Fe, New Mexico, on
2.5 acres of high desert. I can see every sunrise
and sunset, and every moonrise and moonset.
The Milky Way is in my front yard. The kids
are gone, the dogs are old, and life is great.

## About this Book

I created the first edition of this book on a
Mac in Adobe PageMaker 6.5, which I loved.
I designed the pages, wrote the text, did the
production, and produced the index and table
of contents in PageMaker. For this second
edition, I opened the original, eight-year old
PageMaker files in InDesign cs2; the layout,
typographic features, even the index were
intact. Amazing.

The cover was designed, illustrated, and
produced by John Tollett, an incredibly
talented and nice man. He used Photoshop
and InDesign.

Main fonts in the book: Ministry Script, an
OpenType font, for the chapter headings;
Bailey Sans for the headings and subheads;
Adobe Caslon Pro, an OpenType font, for the
body copy. The section openers use Dorchester
Script for the giant initial, Jimbo Standard
Condensed for the large head, and Canterbury
for the small type.